Fourth Edition

PROGRAMED SPELLING DEMONS

George W. Feinstein

Pasadena City College

Prentice Hall, Upper Saddle River, New Jersey 07458

Library of Congress Cataloging-in-Publication Data

Feinstein, George W.
    Programed spelling demons / George W. Feinstein. — 4th ed.
       p.   cm.
    Includes index.
    ISBN 0-13-255621-9
    1. English language—Orthography and spelling—Programed
instructions. I. Title.
PE1145.4.F45   1998
428.1—dc20
                                97-7663
                                    CIP

Editor-in-chief: *Charlyce Jones-Owen*
Acquisition editor: *Maggie Barbieri*
Editorial assistant: *Joan Polk*
Managing editor: *Bonnie Biller*
Production liaison: *Fran Russello*
Editorial/production supervision: *Publications Development Company of Texas*
Prepress & manufacturing buyer: *Mary Ann Gloriande*
Cover designer: *Bruce Kenselaar*
Marketing manager: *Rob Mejia*

This book was set in 10/11 point New Century Schoolbook by Publications Development Company of Texas and was printed and bound by Banta Company. The cover was printed by Banta Company.

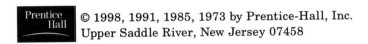

© 1998, 1991, 1985, 1973 by Prentice-Hall, Inc.
Upper Saddle River, New Jersey 07458

Printed in the United States of America

10 9 8

ISBN 0-13-255621-9

Prentice-Hall International (UK) Limited, *London*
Prentice-Hall of Australia Pty. Limited, *Sydney*
Prentice-Hall Canada Inc., *Toronto*
Prentice-Hall Hispanoamericana, S.A., *Mexico*
Prentice-Hall of India Private Limited, *New Delhi*
Prentice-Hall of Japan, Inc., *Tokyo*
Prentice-Hall Asia Pte. Ltd., *Singapore*
Editora Prentice-Hall do Brasil, Ltda., *Rio de Janeiro*

Contents

Preface

A housewife was horrified when her little Barbara came home from school and proudly announced: "Today we learned how to make babies."

"W-what do you mean?"

"We drop the *y* and add *ies*."

Good for Barbara! She has now also learned how to make *cities, stories, armies, navies,* and *libraries.* She is mastering useful rules and useful words, and that is as it should be.

Some spelling programs emphasize "hard" words—like *irascible, hemorrhage, pharyngitis, syzygy*—the breed of words used in national spelling bees to make competitors sweat bullets. Unfortunately, you and I use words like that only about once in seven years, and then we'd be fools not to check their spelling in a dictionary anyhow. It's the demons—words like *its, doesn't, business,* and *receive*—that deserve our most serious, eagle-eyed attention. This workbook is designed to help weak spellers, not Rhodes scholar candidates.

Programed Spelling Demons has certain distinctive features:

1. It is basic. It concentrates on those common pesty words which account for a remarkable 90 percent of student spelling errors.

2. It is programed, enabling students to work alone and at their own pace; yet it can be the basis for classroom assignments and testing.

3. It makes use of a phonics approach, focusing on additive doubling, *ie*-or-*ei*, final silent *e*, pronunciation aids, tricky endings, words often confused, plurals, capitals, apostrophes, and basic principles. It may tackle a word like *writing* in the *hoping-hopping* section, later in the final silent *e* chapter, and once again in a review of nasty, blue-ribbon demons.

4. It puts spelling words into sentence contexts.

5. It encourages development of useful spelling rules by the student, but it ignores spelling rules that are riddled by exceptions to exceptions.

6. It offers a preliminary diagnostic test and a final-day comprehensive test, available to the instructor in the Instructor's Manual, so that spelling improvement in the course can be measured.

7. It stresses drill more than theory, because it assumes that basic spelling—the same as typing or knitting—must be made largely automatic.

8. It includes supplementary lists and exercises as a challenge to ambitious students.

9. It presents its material in a simple, natural sequence that involves no drafty page-turning from frame to answer.

10. It is accompanied by pretests, final tests, and review ideas for each chapter, available to the instructor in the Instructor's Manual.

11. It has been polished and improved by use in classes at more than two hundred colleges and universities and is producing extremely favorable results.

12. It can be used by college students, high school students, a lighthouse-keeper; the only prerequisite is a talent for misspelling words.

Four chapters entitled "Fight Those Demons!" are new in this fourth edition. They are spaced at intervals among other chapters, rather than consecutively, for variety and impact. Many chapters of the prior edition have been retained, with some changes in tests and quizzes.

ACKNOWLEDGMENTS

I intended to thank a gargantuan list of helpful people, but to find space I'd have to cut two chapters from this spelling manual. I will, therefore, be *brief* (*i* before *e* . . .).

I'm especially grateful to four reviewers whose kind words I'll frame as soon as I find some little nails. Those critics are Professors Emily Bluemer (Baker College), Karen Houck (Bellevue Community College), Janice M. Heiges (Northern Virginia Community College), and Theria M. Beverly (Pima Community College).

For high-octane suggestions I also thank Professors Adeline Bingham, Joanne E. Cooper, Mary Alice Hawkins, Mary E. Kreiter, Nancy Hubart-Lowe, Ann R. Morton, Anne Dye Phillips, Burton L. Schweitzer, Ruth E. L. Sherwin, Jean Stephens, and John A. White; and Prentice-Hall Editors Maggie Barbieri, Mary Land, and Joan Polk.

I dedicate this spelling manual to Edith, my *adorable* (*adore* drops the *e* before the suffix *able*) wife.

HOW TO USE THIS MANUAL

1. Cover the answers at the left side of each page with a strip of paper or with your hand.

2. Take up one "frame," or numbered box, at a time.

3. Note carefully any spelling words, explanations, or directions at the beginning of a frame. Have a dictionary near you and look up any term that is not completely clear.

4. Fill in all the blanks of a frame with complete correct spellings, choices, or other answers as indicated.

5. After finishing the whole frame, uncover enough of the key at the left to check your answers. The answer key is numbered the same as the frame and will be found in front of the following frame.

6. If your answers are correct, go on to the next frame.

7. If you have made an error, be sure to correct it. Go back, if necessary, and study the explanations again before you go on. Any word that gives you special spelling trouble—whether in this manual or in your English compositions—should be entered into your Personal List of Demons at the end of this book. Later you will review your personal demons.

8. Complete an entire quiz or entire review test—the same as with each frame—before you check or grade your answers to it.

9. Write neatly and clearly. The act of careful writing, as well as the repetition, will help the learning process.

10. Take additional chapter pretests and review tests as your teacher decides, based on the Instructor's Manual.

1

Phonics: Common Patterns

IN THIS CHAPTER

COVER THIS COLUMN

1   **candid**   **distrust**   **twin**

Read these words aloud, sounding out each letter.

admit	crafts	flank	spanking
blending	damp	fragment	twin
candid	distrust	grasp	vivid

Write *true* or *false*.

a. Each sound in these words is represented by one particular letter.

_____

b. Some English words are spelled just the way they sound. _____

1

1 a. true b. true	**2** church sheep Our alphabet is short. Therefore, some sounds are spelled out by a combination of two letters—such as *sh, ch, th*—called a *digraph*. Digraphs *ch* and *sh*: Copy each word two times. *ch*ildren ——————— ——————— ca*sh* ——————— ——————— *ch*ur*ch* ——————— ——————— *sh*eep ——————— ——————— tea*ch*er ——————— ——————— *sh*oes ——————— ———————
2 [copy]	**3** Write the words in full. On Sunday the ——————— [c–ild–n] put on their new ——————— [s–o–s] and went to ——————— [c–urc–].
3 children shoes church	**4** Write the words in full. a. Said the shepherd: "I've always herded ——————— [s–ep]—and the job's not ba-a-ad." b. I paid my karate ——————— [t–e–c–r] a compliment, but he wanted me to pay ——————— [cas–].
4 a. sheep b. teacher, cash	**5** quarrel theory Combinations *qu* and *th*: Copy each word two times. *qu*arrel ——————— ——————— bo*th* ——————— ——————— *qu*eer ——————— ——————— *th*eory ——————— ——————— *qu*ick ——————— ——————— tru*th* ——————— ———————
5 [copy]	**6** Write the words in full. Sue insisted my ——————— [t–e–ry] that the moon is made of green cheese was ——————— [q–er]—so we had our first ——————— [q–r–l].
6 theory queer quarrel	**7** Write the words in full. Big Ben was ——————— [q–i–k] with his fists, and that's the ——————— [tru–]; but he lost his last fight when Mary hit him with ——————— [bot–] of her crutches.

7 quick truth both	**8** **QUIZ** Write the words in full. a. To make a wool sweater, you have to clip a _____ [s–ep]. b. The _____ [q–ar–l] began when one of the _____ [c–ild–n] dropped hot chocolate on my white tennis _____ [s–o–s]. c. I asked our plumber not to hold back the _____ [tru–] and to give me his _____ [c–n–d] opinion of Einstein's _____ [t–e–ry] of relativity. d. My _____ [te–c–r] gave a _____ [sp–k–ng] to the wrong _____ [tw–n]. e. Some _____ [cas–] was missing, and Lefty felt a deep _____ [di–tr–st] for the poker player with the _____ [q–i–k] fingers.

8
 	
a. sheep
b. quarrel,
    children,
    shoes
c. truth,
    candid,
    theory
d. teacher,
    spanking,
    twin
e. cash,
    distrust,
    quick
	9 **cigar** **giant**
	
	The letter *c* usually sounds like *k (cash, company)*, but *c* gets an *s* sound when it is followed by *e, i,* or *y*.
	The letter *g* usually has a hard sound *(gas, grocery)*, but *g* gets a *j* sound when it is followed by *e, i,* or *y*.
	
	Combinations *ce, ci, cy, ge, gi, gy:* Copy each word two times.
	
	*ce*nt _____ _____ hu*ge* _____ _____
	
	*ci*gar _____ _____ *gi*ant _____ _____
	
	*cy*clone _____ _____ ener*gy* _____ _____

9 [copy]	**10** Write the words in full. The _____ [c–c–one] dropped a _____ [hug–] cow into our petunia bed.
10 cyclone huge	**11** Write the words in full. Smoke a _____ [g–nt] _____ [c–g–r] and it won't give you a _____ [c–nt] worth of _____ [en–rg–].

11 giant cigar cent energy	**12** phobia chronic Words that come to us from the Greek language are often spelled with *ph* for the sound of *f*, and *ch* for the sound of *k*. Digraphs *ch* and *ph*: Copy each word two times. a*ch*e _____ _____ *ch*aracter _____ _____ *ch*ronic _____ _____ ne*ph*ew _____ _____ *ph*obia _____ _____ tele*ph*one _____ _____
12 [copy]	**13** Write the words in full. My _____ [nep–w] at college has a strange _____ [p–bia]. He thinks it's bad luck to call his mother on the _____ [t–l–p–ne] except to ask for money.
13 nephew phobia telephone	**14** Write the words in full. Does Joe have reliable _____ [c–r–c–t–r]? Yes, he's a _____ [c–nic] alcoholic, and his smoking will make your head _____ [ac–]—you can rely on that.
14 character chronic ache	**15** what when which A common combination is *wh*. If you become a news reporter, you'll fill the air with *wh* words. The combination *wh* is used most often at the _____ [beginning/end] of a word. Combination *wh*: Copy each word two times. *wh*at _____ _____ *wh*en _____ _____ *wh*ich _____ _____
15 beginning [copy]	**16** Write the words in full. I'm taking an antibiotic _____ [w–ch] is very powerful. I don't know _____ [w–t] it's called, but _____ [w–n] I sneeze I always cure somebody.

16

which
what
when

Write the words in full.

a. Wow! I met a friendly stranger near the _____ [gr–c–ry], and I fooled him into letting me buy a _____ [hug–] diamond for only twenty dollars _____ [cas–].

b. My _____ [nep–w] picked up a _____ [c–g–r] butt from the gutter, and now he has a _____ [–ron–c] _____ [ac–] in his back.

c. I have a terrible _____ [p–ob–a] that when I take a bath the _____ [tel–p–ne] will ring or a _____ [g–ant] _____ [c–lone] will hit the house.

d. The _____ [c–mp–ny] employer wouldn't let me use the compliment in my fortune cookie as a _____ [c–r–ter] reference.

e. The editor asked _____ [w–at] happened, _____ [w–n] it happened—and why in blazes the reporter didn't have enough _____ [en–r–g–] to get the bloody facts.

17

a. grocery,
   huge,
   cash
b. nephew,
   cigar,
   chronic,
   ache
c. phobia,
   telephone,
   giant,
   cyclone
d. company,
   character
e. what,
   when,
   energy

---

18   **fight**   **light**   **night**

A common spelling pattern is *ight* (pronounced the same as *ite*).
Copy each word once.

blight _____   night _____

delight _____   right _____

fight   _____   sight _____

light   _____   slight _____

might   _____   tight _____

18

[copy]

19

Fill in the blanks with words that use the *ight* pattern.

I thought the jungle _____ [f–] _____ [m–] last all _____ [n–]. Somehow it didn't seem _____ [r–] to _____ [f–] without a _____ [l–].

---

19 fight might night right fight light	**20** Continue as in frame 19. The enemy tied me _____ [t–], and later my rescuers said, "You're a sorry _____ [s–]."
20 tight sight	**21** Continue as in frame 19. To my _____ [del–], though I looked like a _____ [bl–], the damage to me was _____ [sl–].
21 delight blight slight	**22** **bought** **thought** **sought** Another common pattern is *ought*. Copy each word once. bought _____ ought _____ thought _____ brought _____ sought _____ wrought _____ fought _____
22 [copy]	**23** Fill in the blanks with words that use the *ought* pattern. I always _____ [s–] a bargain; so without a second _____ [th–] I _____ [b–] the two elephants for the price of one.
23 sought thought bought	**24** Continue as in frame 23. The two elephants _____ [f–] as I _____ [br–] them into our kitchen.
24 fought brought	**25** Continue as in frame 23. Maybe I _____ [–t] not to have _____ [b–] those elephants. My little bargain _____ [wr–] a big disaster.

25 ought bought wrought	**26** could should would a. The words *could*, *should*, and *would* all end with the same four letters, namely, _____ . b. Two words that rhyme with *could* are _____ and _____ .
26 a. *ould* b. *should,* *would*	**27** Copy the following sentences two times. Should we dance? I would if I could. _____ _____
27 [copy]	**28** Write the words in full. I _____ [w–d] do my rabbit trick now if I _____ [c–d], but I don't think I _____ [sh–d] because I just washed my hare.
28 would could should	**29** Write the words in full. a. You _____ [sh–d] chop wood; then you _____ [c–d] warm yourself twice. b. Newspapers _____ [c–d] and _____ [sh–d]—be made of cellophane, so that family members _____ [w–d] see each other at breakfast.

29
 	
a. should,
    could
b. could,
    should,
    would
	30 QUIZ
	
	Write the words in full.
	
	a. Max _____ [tho–t] that our city _____ [sh–d] have a strict law against gambling, and he bet me ten to one that such a law _____ [w–d] pass.
	
	b. I believe your tomcat had a _____ [sl–t] _____ [fi–t] the other _____ [ni–t]. A cat _____ [o–t] to have two ears.
	
	c. Little Randy said that the sun _____ [sh–d] shine at _____ [ni–t] when we need the _____ [li–t]. He _____ [c–d] be _____ [ri–t].

d. As soon as I _____ [bo–t] my airplane tickets, I felt a surge of panic. I _____ [fo–t] my fear. And what had _____ [br–t] it all on? It was the _____ [si–t] of those busy life insurance policy machines.

30

a. thought,
   should,
   would
b. slight,
   fight,
   night,
   ought
c. should,
   night,
   light,
   could,
   right
d. bought,
   fought,
   brought,
   sight

31

Enter any words that you misspelled in this chapter into your Personal List of Demons in the Appendix.

REVIEW TEST: CHAPTER 1

Fill in the blanks with words studied in this chapter.

1. Hank's heart was _____ [li–t] as a feather; that's why he needed a transplant.

2. When my boss smokes a _____ [c–g–r], I can't see the typewriter in front of me.

3. Tom's flea circus, one _____ [mi–t] say, started from scratch.

4. The pastor of the _____ [c–urc–] put up a sign: "Keep off the lawn. This means Thou."

5. To play basketball, it helps to be a _____ [g–ant].

6. The weatherman _____ [tho–t] it would be sunny if it didn't rain.

7. A nickel might roll under the bed, but _____ [cas–] doesn't go far nowadays.

8. Joe _____ [bo–t] a shampoo called Noodle Soup.

9. He's a public official, _____ [w–ic–] is why he doesn't work.

10. To be hit by a _____ [c–clon–] is an uplifting experience.

11. During the war, Elmer _____ [fo–t] hard, but still he had to go.

12. More important than money is _____ [c–r–ct–r].

13. Youthful energy is wasted, alas, on _____ [c–ild–n].

14. From students a _____ [te–c–r] also learns something—that they don't study.

15. Scrooge was a _____ [c–ron–c] penny pincher and faultfinder—and those were his better traits.

16. Fudd lived in a tent _____ [w–n] he was a baby, so his head grew to a point.

17. The doctor gave me pills to increase my _____ [en–rg–], but I was too tired to take them.

18. An actor wants flattery, not the _____ [tru–].

19. My niece and my _____ [nep–w] invented dog food that tastes like a mail carrier's leg.

20. The Statue of Liberty is a thrilling _____ [si–t].

21. As the bride and groom left the altar, they began to _____ [q–r–l].

22. The school board warned Scopes not to monkey with Darwin's _____ [t–e–ry] of evolution.

23. When you hunt elephants, you _____ [sh–u–d] make a noise like a peanut.

24. Bell invented the _____ [t–l–p–on–] so his daughter would have dates.

25. If only Noah _____ [w–u–d] have swatted those two mosquitoes!

KEY TO REVIEW TEST

Check your test answers with the following key. Deduct 4% per error from a possible 100%.

1. light	6. thought	11. fought	16. when	21. quarrel
2. cigar	7. cash	12. character	17. energy	22. theory
3. might	8. bought	13. children	18. truth	23. should
4. church	9. which	14. teacher	19. nephew	24. telephone
5. giant	10. cyclone	15. chronic	20. sight	25. would

Score: _____ %

Now, here are three things to do:

1. If you misspelled any words in this review test, be sure to enter them in your Personal List of Demons in the Appendix.

2. Go back and study the frames that deal with the words that you misspelled.

3. Take the final test on this chapter, to be given by your instructor (Instructor's Manual).

IMPORTANT: From now on, do these same three things at the end of each chapter that you study.

2

Words Often Confused I

IN THIS CHAPTER

1. accept	5. passed	9. then	13. too	17. your
2. except	6. past	10. there	14. two	18. you're
3. its	7. than	11. they're	15. who's	
4. it's	8. their	12. to	16. whose	

COVER THIS COLUMN	**1** **to** **too** **two**
	to: toward, until; also used before a verb, as in "*to* sing." "Frank went *to* the barn *to* feed the pigs."
	too: more than enough; also. "That basketball center is *too* short, and he's *too* slow, *too*."
	two: 2. "In *two* seconds I lost *two* teeth."
	Copy each phrase two times. (Memorize spelling whenever you copy the phrases in this manual.)
	to write _____ _____
	too busy _____ _____
	two women _____ _____
1 [copy]	**2** Write *to, too,* or *two*. Shorty's shoes are _____ big. [Means "more than enough."]

2 too	**3** Write *to, too,* or *two.* a. Grandpa made a one-way trip ——————— the graveyard. [Means "toward."] b. Cut my onion pie in ——————— . [Means "2."]
3 a. to b. two	**4** Write *to, too,* or *two.* a. Bill fights in a crouch, so he won't have ——————— far ——————— fall. b. At midnight Tony is going ——————— play ——————— pieces on his tuba.
4 a. too, to b. to, two	**5** Write *to, too,* or *two.* It's ——————— bad that a woman may have ——————— be ——————— times as good as a man ——————— win a top job.
5 too to two to	**6** **QUIZ** Write *to, too,* or *two.* a. Which word means "toward"? ——————— b. Which word means "also"? ——————— c. Which word means "more than enough"? ——————— d. Which word means "2"? ——————— e. Which word is used before verbs? ———————
6 a. *to* b. *too* c. *too* d. *two* e. *to*	**7** Write *to, too,* or *two.* Uncle Casper drove ——————— fast ——————— traffic school and hit ——————— dogs.
7 too to two	**8** Write *to, too,* or *two.* The old man walked ——————— miles ——————— the river ——————— drown himself, then decided that the water was ——————— cold.

8 two to to too	**9** Write *to, too,* or *two.* a. Is it possible _____ be _____ rich? b. Lefty, this town is _____ small for the _____ of us. c. The quake hit at *1:58 A.M., also.* In other words, it hit at _____ _____ _____, _____.
9 a. to, too b. too, two c. two to two, too	**10** **its** **it's** *its* (shows ownership). "The bear wore *its* fur coat." *it's* (contraction): it is. "*It's* a pretty good fit." Copy each phrase two times. Try its motor. _____ _____ Now it's paid. _____ _____
10 [copy]	**11** Write *its* or *it's.* My shoe has a nail in _____ heel. [HINT: Try to substitute "it is" in the blank—if it makes sense, write *it's.* Otherwise, write *its.* Now, does "a nail in *it is* heel" make sense? _____]
11 its no	**12** Write *its* or *it's.* An army uniform comes in two sizes: Either _____ too big or _____ too small. [Try saying "Either *it is* too big. . . ." Do those words make sense? _____ If so, write the contraction for "it is."]
12 it's it's yes	**13** Write *its* or *it's.* Keep trying the "it is" test for *it's.* I hope that _____ not time for that airplane above us to drop _____ bombs.
13 it's its	**14** Write *its* or *it's.* My cat is chasing _____ tail, but _____ not running fast enough.

14 its it's	**15** Write *its* or *it's*. My jalopy needs work on _____ body, _____ motor, and _____ transmission; but otherwise _____ a very good car.
15 its its its it's	**16** **QUIZ** Write *its* or *it's*. a. The word _____ can only mean "it is." b. The word _____ can only show ownership. c. The baby hollered for _____ bottle. d. My tomcat lost _____ ear in a lovers' quarrel. e. Yes, _____ a giraffe with a sore throat. f. Help! This bathroom lost _____ doorknob.

16
 	
a. *it's*
b. *its*
c. its
d. its
e. it's
f. its
	17 **your** **you're**
	
	your (shows ownership). "Mr. Bell, *your* machine will never work."
	you're: you are. "Mr. Bell, *you're* a genius!"
	
	Copy each phrase two times.
	
	See your professor. _____
	
	  _____
	
	You're beautiful. _____
	
	  _____

17 [copy]	**18** Write *your* or *you're*. Don't worry, but _____ parachute should have opened by now. [Hint: Try to substitute "you are" in the blank—if it makes sense, write *you're*. Otherwise, write *your*. Does "*you are* parachute" make sense? _____]
18 your no	**19** Write *your* or *you're*. If _____ seasick, please don't lean on my new suit. [Try saying "If *you are* seasick. . . ." Do these words make sense? _____ If so, write the contraction for "you are."]

19 you're yes	**20** Keep trying the "you are" test for *you're*. Cut _____ artery and _____ in trouble.
20 your you're	**21** Write *your* or *you're*. ". . . and I'm telling you, Columbus, that _____ crazy, and _____ three ships will fall off the edge of the earth."
21 you're your	**22** Write *your* or *you're*. Then Madame Lazonga told me—and _____ not going to believe this: "I can read by _____ palm, sonny, that _____ short of soap."
22 you're your you're	**23** **QUIZ** Write *your* or *you're*. a. The word _____ can only show ownership. b. The word _____ can only mean "you are." c. I saw _____ picture on the post office wall. d. Give Butch _____ wallet, or _____ dead! e. When _____ playing ping-pong, keep _____ mouth closed.
23 a. *your* b. *you're* c. your d. your, you're e. you're, your	**24** **who's** **whose** *who's:* who is. "*Who's* on first?" *whose* (shows ownership). "*Whose* hair is swimming in my soup?" Copy each phrase two times. Who's losing? _____ _____ Whose cigarette? _____ _____
24 [copy]	**25** Write *who's* or *whose*. Find out _____ truck ran over my tulips. [HINT: Try to substitute "who is" in the blank—if it makes sense, write *who's*. Otherwise, write *whose*. Does the phrase "*who is* truck" make sense? _____]

25 whose no	**26** Write *who's* or *whose*. Tell me _____ pitching and I'll tell you _____ team will win. [Try saying "*who is* pitching." If these words make sense, write the contraction *who's;* otherwise, write the possessive *whose.* Also try "*who is* team."]
26 who's whose	**27** Keep trying the "who is" test for *who's.* "Speak up," said the policeman. "_____ your father, _____ your friend, and _____ car are you driving?"
27 Who's who's whose	**28** Write *who's* or *whose*. Show me a student _____ weak in spelling and I'll show you a student _____ themes get beautiful *D's* and *F's*.
28 who's whose	**29** **QUIZ** Write *who's* or *whose*. a. The word _____ shows ownership. b. The word _____ can only mean "who is." c. I wonder _____ kissing Velma now. d. I wonder _____ golf ball hit my head. e. Dad loves Little Orphan Annie, _____ smart as a whip and _____ eyes look like doughnuts.
29 a. *whose* b. *who's* c. who's d. whose e. who's, whose	**30** **their** **there** **they're** *their* (shows ownership). "That's *their* goat." Both *their* and *heir* suggest ownership. *there:* in that place. "I stood *there.*" Both *there* and *here* suggest a place. *they're:* they are. "I hope *they're* mushrooms." You can substitute *they are* for *they're.* Copy each phrase two times. It's their business. _____ _____ Yes, they're there. _____ _____

30 [copy]	**31** Write *their*, *there*, or *they're*. Over _____ is a nearsighted hen sitting on a snowball. [Means "in that place."]
31 there	**32** Write *their*, *there*, or *they're*. a. Our fat relatives ate _____ turkey in October. [Shows owner-ship.] b. Now _____ hungry. [Means "they are."]
32 a. their b. they're	**33** Write *their*, *there*, or *they're*. a. Don't insult them! _____ my friends. b. Here is my pig, and _____ is _____ pig.
33 a. They're b. there, their	**34** Write *their*, *there*, or *they're*. a. The word _____ means "in that place." b. The word _____ means "they are." c. The word _____ shows ownership. d. Kids are skating _____ on the ice rink, and _____ falling on _____ bottoms.
34 a. *there* b. *they're* c. *their* d. there, they're, their	**35** Write *their*, *there*, or *they're*. a. Big Jim's pallbearers say _____ tired. b. I hope _____ very happy in _____ pretty cottage over _____ next to the swamp.
35 a. they're b. they're, their, there	**36** Write *their*, *there*, or *they're*. Those people sitting _____ —if _____ waiting to see the psychiatrist, they should have _____ heads examined.

36

there
they're
their

Write in full the words we have studied.

_____ a. [You–] smart.   _____ f. [The–] late.

_____ b. [Who–] purse?   _____ g. I'm [t–] old.

_____ c. Go [the–] soon.   _____ h. [Who–] that?

_____ d. [It–] a taco.   _____ i. It's [the–] problem.

_____ e. Try [t–] pray.   _____ j. Save [you–] niece.

37

a. You're
b. Whose
c. there
d. It's
e. to
f. They're
g. too
h. Who's
i. their
j. your

---

38   **accept**   **except**

accept (verb): to take or receive. "I'll *accept* a glass of low-fat milk."

except: all but. "Everybody *except* Sam caught the flu." *Except* suggests an
  exception.

Copy this sentence two times.

Boys accept everything except advice.

_____

_____

38

[copy]

39

Write *accept* or *except*.

The whole army is out of step _____ my brother. [An exception.]

39

except

40

Write *accept* (take) or *except* (an exception).

Please _____ this pot of Mama's chicken soup. It will cure anything

_____ flat feet.

40

accept
except

41

Write *accept* or *except*.

You may _____ all his gifts, Nellie, _____ the diamond ring.

If you _____ the ring, you'll have to marry the bum.

41

accept
except
accept

---

42   **QUIZ**

Write *accept* or *except*.

a. To receive is to _____ .

b. Joe won't _____ bribes, _____ big ones.

c. I can resist anything _____ temptation.

d. I'll _____ any job _____ dogcatcher.

e. Should the Trojans _____ this nice wooden horse from the Greeks? Tune in next week.

---

42 a. accept b. accept, except c. except d. accept, except e. accept	**43** **passed** **past** *passed* (verb, past tense of *pass*). "We *passed* the hospital." Notice the verb ending, *ed*. *past:* beyond; earlier. "We walked *past* the hospital during this *past* week." Copy each phrase two times. A year passed. _____ _____ the past year _____ _____
43 [copy]	**44** Write *passed* or *past*. She _____ me as if I had smallpox. [Here *she* is the subject of a verb, and the verb ends in *ed*.]
44 passed	**45** Write *passed* or *past*. Keep looking for subject-and-verb *(ed)* combinations. In the _____ semester, Elmer _____ no courses except Basketball 1A.
45 past passed	**46** Write *passed* or *past*. Buster has now _____ the Pearly Gates, and all his troubles belong to the _____ .
46 passed past	**47** Write *passed* or *past*. Patsy _____ a few bad checks, and so she has _____ these _____ years in a few well-built jails.
47 passed passed past	**48** **QUIZ** Write *passed* or *past*. a. The verb _____ is the _____ tense of *pass*. b. The bus _____ us in a cloud of fumes.

c. Look ahead. The _____ is history.

d. Bill lost a quart of blood this _____ week and _____ out.

48

a. *passed,* past
b. passed
c. past
d. past, passed

---

49   **than**   **then**

than (used in comparisons). "My weeds are taller *than* yours."

then: at that time. "*Then* I froze my ears."

Copy each phrase two times.

bigger than you _____ _____

now and then   _____ _____

49

[copy]

50

Write *than* or *then.*

a. I sang, and _____ they booed. [Means "at that time."]

b. One hair on your head is better _____ two in the sink.

50

a. then
b. than

51

Write *than* or *then.*

His job _____ was bigger _____ mine. He washed elephants

now and _____ .

51

then
than
then

52

Write *than* or *then.*

Grandpa was thinner _____ . In fact, he was skinnier _____

_____ a garden rake.

52

then
then
than

---

53   **QUIZ**

Write *than* or *then.*

a. The word _____ often suggests time.

b. The word _____ suggests a comparison.

c. Zeke is somewhat smarter _____ his cow.

d. Poets went hungry _____ , the same as now.

e. Kay borrowed my pot, _____ cooked my goose.

53

a. *then*
b. *than*
c. than
d. then
e. then

54

Enter any words that you misspelled in this chapter into your Personal List of Demons in the Appendix.

REVIEW TEST: CHAPTER 2

Fill in the blanks with words studied in this chapter.

1. If _____ [you–] poor, the doctor cures you faster.

2. The monkey hung by _____ [it–] tail.

3. Mrs. Bliss's kisses were sweeter _____ [th–] wine.

4. I wouldn't enter _____ [you–] room without a tetanus shot.

5. Lucy is one woman _____ [who–] afraid of the big bad wolf.

6. After Dad _____ [pas–] away, our town brewery went broke.

7. I can't catch fish if the worms aren't doing _____ [th–] best.

8. Consult _____ [t–] lawyers and you get three legal opinions.

9. The salt is right _____ [th–] under your nose.

10. We've read _____ [you–] poetry—on a barn wall.

11. To make an omelet, you have _____ [t–] crack an egg.

12. The cannibal _____ [who–] on a diet eats only midgets.

13. Our jewels! You say _____ [the–] all fakes?

14. Sam says he's _____ [t–] sick to go to the doctor.

15. Bob makes blotters—_____ [it–] absorbing work.

16. The fellow at my left _____ [pas–] me a meatball.

17. If _____ [you–] a sailor, I'm Christopher Columbus.

18. Rip could do anything _____ [–cept] make money.

19. I wonder _____ [who–] elbow is in my neck.

20. I had to _____ [–cept] the gangster's insult.

21. The lawn I mowed was bigger _____ [th–n] Kansas.

22. Even a porcupine has _____ [it–] good points.

23. The atheist hurried _____ [pas–] the church.

24. The cowboys were picking _____ [the–] teeth.

25. And _____ [th–n] we added the garlic.

KEY TO REVIEW TEST

Check your test answers with the following key. Deduct 4% per error from a possible 100%.

1. you're	**6.** passed	**11.** to	**16.** passed	**21.** than
2. its	**7.** their	**12.** who's	**17.** you're	**22.** its
3. than	**8.** two	**13.** they're	**18.** except	**23.** past
4. your	**9.** there	**14.** too	**19.** whose	**24.** their
5. who's	**10.** your	**15.** it's	**20.** accept	**25.** then

Score: _____%

3

Words Often Confused II

IN THIS CHAPTER

COVER THIS COLUMN	**1** a an

Let us examine how *a* and *an* are used.

a big egg	an egg
a fool	an old fool
a heavy man	an honorable man [the *h* here is silent]
a rat	an accident

a. **RULE: We use *a* before words that begin with a _____ [consonant/vowel] sound.** Vowels are *a, e, i, o, u,* and *y;* consonants are the other letters—like *b, f, g, k, l, p, r.*

b. **RULE: We use *an* before words that begin with a _____ [consonant/vowel] sound.** Notice, though, that the letters *u* and *y* sometimes have a consonant **sound:** "a unit, a yard."

1 a. consonant b. vowel	**2** Write *a* or *an*. For _____ ticket to this big rock concert, you'll be charged only _____ arm and _____ leg.
2 a an a	**3** Write *a* or *an*. In _____ luxury motel, Sam was attacked by _____ spider that was _____ inch long.
3 a a an	**4** Write *a* or *an*. Tex cut down _____ beautiful tree with _____ axe and made himself _____ ugly fence.
4 a an an	**5** **QUIZ** Write *a* or *an*. a. We write _____ before words like *fist, pill,* and *lonely.* b. We write _____ before words like *art, ox,* and *idiot.* c. For thirty cents the hobo got _____ cup of coffee, _____ overcoat, and _____ umbrella.
5 a. *a* b. *an* c. a, an, an	**6** **advice *(noun)* advise *(verb)*** Copy each phrase two times, including the capital letters. adVICE about ICE _____ _____ WISE men adVISE _____ _____
6 [copy]	**7** Write *advice* or *advise*. a. Please _____ . [Verb; rhymes with *wise.*] b. I need cheap legal _____ . [Noun; rhymes with *ice.*]
7 a. advise b. advice	**8** Write *advice* or *advise*. My _____ ? Get a minister to _____ you.

8

advice
advise

---

9   QUIZ

Write *advice* or *advise*.

a. The word _____ rhymes with *ice;* the word _____ rhymes with *wise.*

b. I _____ poet Jim to marry a rich widow.

c. Don't _____ poets and artists; they want compliments, not _____ .

9

a. *advice,*
   advise
b. advise
c. advise,
   advice

---

10   **affect**   **effect**

affect (verb): to influence. "Crimes *affect* us."
effect (noun): result. "Heat has a bad *effect.*"
effect (verb): to cause or bring about. "Let's *effect* a compromise."

Copy each phrase two times.

will affect me   _____   _____

a strange effect _____   _____

effect a change   _____   _____

10

[copy]

11

Write *affect* or *effect*.

a. High taxes _____ us. [Verb; means "to influence."]

b. Alcohol has a mind-crippling _____ . [Noun; means "result."]

c. We must _____ an improvement. [Verb; means "to bring about."]

11

a. affect
b. effect
c. effect

12

Write *affect* or *effect*.

Wars _____ everybody, and the general _____ is tragic.

12

affect
effect

13

Write *affect* or *effect*.

a. Television has its _____ on public opinion.

b. Kisses can _____ your pulse rate.

c. My apple to teacher didn't _____ my grades.

13 a. effect b. affect c. affect	**14** QUIZ Write *affect* or *effect*. a. Study the laws of cause and _____. b. Animal fats _____ your arteries. c. Slim tried to _____ an escape through the ventilator. d. Carrots have a good _____ on eyesight. Did you ever see a rabbit wearing glasses?
14 a. effect b. affect c. effect d. effect	**15** aisle isle Copy each phrase two times. church aisle _____ _____ Pacific isle _____ _____ The first three letters of both *isle* and island are _____.
15 [copy] *isl*	**16** Write *aisle* or *isle*. a. I stumbled along the dark theater _____. b. A small island is known as an _____. c. The bridegroom came down the _____ like a condemned man.
16 a. aisle b. isle c. aisle	**17** altar alter Copy each phrase two times. altar ceremony _____ alter a word _____
17 [copy]	**18** Write *altar* or *alter*. a. His fists may _____ the shape of my nose. b. The rabbi blessed the couple at the _____. c. The gambler knelt at the _____ , hoping to _____ his luck.

18

a. alter
b. altar
c. altar, alter

19   QUIZ

Write in full the words we have studied.

_____ a. [alt–] a plan

_____ b. movie [–sle]

_____ c. need [adv–]

_____ d. bad [–fect]

_____ e. eat [a–] egg

_____ f. [adv–] us

19

a. alter
b. aisle
c. advice
d. effect
e. an
f. advise

20   angel   angle

Angel needs the *ge* combination to give it a *j* sound; *angle* doesn't.

Copy each phrase two times.

a cute angel   _____   _____

acute angle   _____   _____

20

[copy]

21

Write *angel* or *angle*.

a.   I'd be an _____ , but I can't play a harp.

b.   The letter *g* in _____ sounds like the *g* in *gas*.

21

a. angel
b. *angle*

22

Write *angel* or *angle*.

a.   The driver made a right-_____ turn, and bam!—he's an

_____ in heaven.

b.   The *ge* in _____ sounds like *j*.

c.   "You're an _____ , Babe," growled Scarface, "but what's your

_____ ?"

22

a. angle,
   angel
b. *angel*
c. angel,
   angle

23   berth   birth

A b*erth* is a b*ed* on a train. Notice the *e*'s.

Copy each phrase two times.

lower berth   _____   _____

birth of a baby   _____   _____

23 [copy]	**24** Write *berth* or *birth*. a. Get a _____ certificate—or you're dead. b. A pullman bed is known as a _____ .
24 a. birth b. berth	**25** Write *berth* or *birth*. a. The train crash threw me from my _____ . b. Our cat Bill gave _____ to five kittens. c. Olga gave _____ to twins in the upper _____ .
25 a. berth b. birth c. birth, berth	**26**　　　　**brake**　　　　**break** Copy each phrase two times. a brake job　_____　_____ break the glass　_____　_____
26 [copy]	**27** Write *brake* or *break*. Step on the _____ , or you'll _____ your neck.
27 brake break	**28** Write *brake* or *break*. a. The train is stopped by an air _____ . b. The garage checked my emergency _____ ; then I had to _____ a twenty-dollar bill. c. A tough _____ ! One skier happened to _____ his leg in two places—Colorado and Switzerland.
28 a. brake b. brake, 　break c. break, 　break	**29**　　　　　　　　　　**QUIZ** Write in full the words we have studied. _____ a. upper [b–rth]　　　_____ d. [br–] an egg _____ b. 45° [ang–]　　　_____ e. winged [ang–] _____ c. a [br–] pedal　　　_____ f. [b–rth] pains

29

a. berth
b. angle
c. brake
d. break
e. angel
f. birth

---

30   breath *(noun)*   breathe *(verb)*

Copy each phrase two times.

a deep breath   _____ _____

breathe deeply   _____ _____

30

[copy]

31

Write *breath* or *breathe*.

a. My sweetheart has sweet _____ .

b. If you ate onions, don't _____ on me.

31

a. breath
b. breathe

32

Write *breath* or *breathe*.

a. To _____ first-class smog, try Los Angeles.

b. A lovely view! It took my _____ away.

32

a. breathe
b. breath

33

Write *breath* or *breathe*.

a. "Take a deep _____ , Joe," said Dr. Fumble. "Just _____

deep. It hurts you to _____ ? Well, I'll stop that."

b. I took a big _____ of fresh sea air (what a pleasure to _____
it!), and my lungs said, "What's that stuff?"

33

a. breath,
   breathe,
   breathe
b. breath,
   breathe

---

34   capital   capitol

The *capitol* is a legislative building or statehouse (the dome is often "*O*-shaped).
Use *capital* for all other meanings, including *capital* city.

Copy each phrase twice, including the capital *O*.

capital idea   _____

               _____

capitOl dOme   _____

               _____

34 [copy]	**35** Write *capital* or *capitol*. a. To build a hot dog factory you need _____. b. The statehouse with an *O*-dome is our _____.
35 a. capital b. capitol	**36** Write *capital* or *capitol*. a. Mike wrote "POVERTY IS INEXPENSIVE" in _____ letters. b. In the _____ building the senators voted to end _____ punishment and to make more H-bombs.
36 a. capital b. capitol, capital	**37** **close** **clothes** **cloths** Copy each phrase two times. Close the door. _____ _____ Wear old clothes. _____ _____ Use wash cloths. _____ _____
37 [copy]	**38** Write *close, clothes,* or *cloths.* Put the two wash _____ in the _____ closet and _____ the door.
38 cloths clothes close	**39** Write *close, clothes,* or *cloths.* a. Buy one red cloth and four blue _____. b. Fritz flapped around in his dad's _____. c. _____ the bathroom door before taking off your _____.
39 a. cloths b. clothes c. Close, clothes	**40** **conscience** **conscious** Religious SCIENCE believes in a CONSCIENCE, that is, one's sense of right and wrong. *Conscious* means "awake, aware." Copy each phrase two times, including the capital letters. his CONSCIENCE _____ _____ He's conscious. _____ _____

40 [copy]	**41** Write *conscience* or *conscious*. You deserted your thirteen children. Are you _____ of doing wrong, or have you no _____ ?
41 conscious conscience	**42** Write *conscience* or *conscious*. a. Ed hit a rock and is still not _____ . b. *Science* is part of the word _____ . c. My painless dentist isn't _____ of my pain.
42 a. conscious b. conscience c. conscious	**43** **QUIZ** Write in full the words we have studied. _____ a. to [cl–] the door _____ b. to [br–] bus fumes _____ c. the [cap–t–l] building _____ d. a clear [consc–] _____ e. a suit of [cl–] _____ f. invests [cap–t–l] _____ g. short of [br–] _____ h. Is he [consc–]?
43 a. close b. breathe c. capitol d. conscience e. clothes f. capital g. breath h. conscious	**44** **consul** **council** **counsel** A *consul* represents his or her country in a foreign city. A *council* is a group that makes decisions. *Counsel* is advice; to *counsel* is to advise. Copy each phrase two times. He's our consul. _____ _____ The council met. _____ _____ I need counsel. _____ _____

44 [copy]	**45** Write *consul, council,* or *counsel.* In Paris, go to the American _____ [means "representative"] for _____ [means "advice"].
45 consul counsel	**46** Write *consul, council,* or *counsel.* a. Chief Wise Fox headed the Indian _____ [means "group that makes decisions"]. b. A Boy Scout who mugs old ladies needs _____. c. The mayor will _____ you after his _____ meeting.
46 a. council b. counsel c. counsel, council	**47** **dairy** **diary** Say *DAIR-y* and *DI-a-ry* five times and notice the difference in the vowel sounds. Copy each phrase two times. dairy cows _____ _____ Keep a diary. _____ _____
47 [copy]	**48** Write *dairy* or *diary.* The _____ farmer kept a _____.
48 dairy diary	**49** **QUIZ** Write *dairy* or *diary.* a. The first syllable of _____ sounds like *die.* b. Send this sour milk back to the _____. c. _____ has two syllables; _____ has three. d. What romantic secrets in Fifi's _____!

49
 	
a. *diary*
b. dairy
c. *Dairy,*
  diary
d. diary
	50 decent descent
	
	DECENT means "proper; in good taste"; deSCENT refers to going down [think of going down an *S*-curve]; or to family origin.
	
	Copy each phrase two times.
	
	decent manners _____
	
	  _____
	
	descent to earth _____
	
	  _____

50 [copy]	**51** Write *decent* or *descent*. Let's make a _____ [means "going down"] into the bargain basement and buy _____ clothes [means "in good taste"].
51 descent decent	**52** Write *decent* or *descent*. I want a _____ wage before I make another _____ into this coal mine.
52 decent descent	**53** Write *decent* or *descent*. a. We accent the first syllable of _____. b. We accent the second syllable of _____. c. One pilot of Irish _____ [means "family origin"] made his _____ by parachute.
53 a. *decent* b. *descent* c. descent, descent	**54** QUIZ Write in full the words we have studied. _____ a. [d–c–nt] manners _____ b. needs [c–n–l] _____ c. [d–ry] butter _____ d. a city [c–n–l] _____ e. steep [d–cent] _____ f. a secret [d–ry]

54

a. decent
b. counsel
c. dairy
d. council
e. descent
f. diary

55　　　　desert　　　　dessert

Note the accents: Let's deSERT him in the DESert, after he eats desSERT. And remember—a *dessert* is full of calories and *s*'s.

Now, copy the following sentence two times.

Desert him in the desert, after he eats dessert.

_____

_____

_____

55

[copy]

56

Write *desert* or *dessert*.

a. Arabs in the _____ ate figs for _____ .

b. What is full of calories and *s*'s? _____ .

56

a. desert,
　 dessert
b. dessert

57

Write *desert* or *dessert*.

a. I don't eat _____ , starting tomorrow.

b. What a rat—to _____ his mother!

c. Don't _____ Ed; he has pies for _____ .

57

a. dessert
b. desert
c. desert,
　 dessert

58　　　　device *(noun)*　　　　devise *(verb)*

Copy each sentence two times, including the capital letters.

This deVICE cuts ICE. _____

_____

The WISE deVISE plans. _____

_____

58

[copy]

59

Write *device* or *devise*.

a. The word _____ rhymes with *ice*.

b. The word _____ rhymes with *wise*.

59

a. *device*
b. *devise*

60

Write *device* or *devise*.

a. Eli Whitney, did you _____ this cotton-picking contraption?

b. An alarm clock is an irritating _____.

c. Please _____ an antismog _____.

60

a. devise
b. device
c. devise, device

---

61   dual   duel

Dual means "double."
A *duel* is a contest.

Copy each phrase two times.

dual pipes   _____

_____

fight a duel   _____

_____

61

[copy]

62

Write *dual* or *duel*.

Twain fought a _____ using water pistols.

62

duel

63

Write *dual* or *duel*.

a. In a _____ of wits, Pete had no weapons.

b. The Red Baron fought the _____ firing _____ [2] cannons.

c. Dingbat had a _____ personality: He'd either hug you or want

to _____ with you.

63

a. duel
b. duel, dual
c. dual, duel

---

64   foreword   forward

A books' FOREWORD is a kind of beFORE WORD, or book introduction.
The word forWARD is a cousin of onWARD and toWARD.

Copy each phrase two times.

foreword of a book   _____

_____

Step forward.   _____

_____

64

[copy]

65

Write *foreword* or *forward*.

a. The historian wrote in the _____ that our nation will go

_____ .

b. Related to *onward* is _____ ; related to *afterword* is

_____ .

65

a. foreword,
    forward
b. *forward,*
    foreword

66

Write *foreword* or *forward*.

a. I ran _____ and fell into a cesspool.

b. Angus read the _____ and fell asleep.

c. Is humankind really marching _____?—so asks the author in

his _____ .

66

a. forward
b. foreword
c. forward,
    foreword

---

67   forth   fourth

Note the *four* in *fourth*. Copy each phrase two times.

and so forth   _____

_____

fourth grade   _____

_____

67

[copy]

68

Write *forth* or *fourth*.

Step _____ . You've won _____ prize.

68

forth
fourth

69

Write *forth* or *fourth*.

a. On his _____ birthday, Melvin got a hernia.

b. Don Quixote went _____ to fight dragons.

c. After the _____ act, the soprano stepped _____
    to accept the roses that she had bought.

69

a. fourth
b. forth
c. fourth,
    forth

---

70   QUIZ

Write in full the words we have studied.

_____ a. [fo–th] floor

_____ b. [des–t] sand

_____ c. a gun [du–l]

_____ d. cheesecake for [des–t]

_____ e. march [for–d]

_____ f. [dev–] a method

_____ g. handy [dev–]

_____ h. burst [fo–th]

_____ i. read the [for–d]

_____ j. [du–l] exhaust pipes

70

a. fourth
b. desert
c. duel
d. dessert
e. forward
f. devise
g. device
h. forth
i. foreword
j. dual

71

Enter any words that you misspelled in this chapter into your Personal List of Demons in the Appendix.

Fill in the blanks with words studied in this chapter.

1. Rabbits don't believe in _____ [b–rth] control.

2. Dad invested our _____ [cap–l] in Florida swamps.

3. Drugs have a harmful _____ [–fect] on athletes.

4. Here lies Cass; he tried to _____ [br–th–] gas.

5. The villain Simon Legree had no _____ [consc–].

6. Invent a _____ [dev–] to catch mice.

7. The tribe ate *a* tuna, *a* sailor, and _____ [–] ox.

8. Do you want fancy waiters or a _____ [d–c–nt] meal?

9. Mike wore his best Sunday _____ [clo–] on Tuesday.

10. Pray! The _____ [br–] pedal is stuck!

11. Salary cuts will _____ [–fect] our life style.

12. Lucky the reader who peeps into Pepys' _____ [d–ry]!

13. Our city _____ [co–n–l] debated garbage pickups.

14. Are you _____ [consc–] of prejudice?

15. Take my _____ [adv–]: Don't order the meatloaf.

16. Burr and Hamilton fought a _____ [du–l].

17. Sonya and Igor are of Russian _____ [d–c–nt].

18. At the movies I sat next to the _____ [–sle].

19. Come _____ [f–th] and be recognized.

20. Quarterbacks often _____ [br–] a few bones.

21. The homeliest baby looks like an _____ [ang–].

22. "Never _____ [alt–r] a paycheck," said the convict.

23. Life can be dull on a small tropical _____ [–sle].

24. The author cites his aims in the _____ [fo–w–rd].

25. Our camel deserted us in the _____ [d–s–rt].

KEY TO REVIEW TEST

Check your test answers with the following key. Deduct 4% per error from a possible 100%.

1. birth	**6.** device	**11.** affect	**16.** duel	**21.** angel
2. capital	**7.** an	**12.** diary	**17.** descent	**22.** alter
3. effect	**8.** decent	**13.** council	**18.** aisle	**23.** isle
4. breathe	**9.** clothes	**14.** conscious	**19.** forth	**24.** foreword
5. conscience	**10.** brake	**15.** advice	**20.** break	**25.** desert

Score: _____ %

4

Words Often Confused III

IN THIS CHAPTER

1. have	9. martial	17. peace	25. shone	33. weak
2. hear	10. moral	18. personal	26. shown	34. weather
3. here	11. morale	19. personnel	27. stake	35. week
4. hole	12. new	20. piece	28. stationary	36. were
5. instance	13. of	21. principal	29. stationery	37. where
6. instants	14. off	22. principle	30. steak	38. whether
7. knew	15. pail	23. role	31. threw	39. whole
8. marital	16. pale	24. roll	32. through	

COVER THIS COLUMN	**1** **have** *(verb)* **of** *(preposition)*
	RULE: Use *have*—not *of*—after ***should, could, would,*** **and** ***must.*** This is a matter of grammar, and good grammar won't damage your theme grades. Read the following sentence aloud twice; then write it twice.
	One *of* you might *have*—could *have*—should *have* gone.
	_____
	_____
	_____
1 [copy]	**2** a. A common auxiliary (helping) verb is _____ [*have/of*]. b. Is it good grammar to use the word *of* after the word *should?* _____

43

2

a. *have*

b. no

3

Write *have* or *of*.

a. The thief must _____ stolen one _____ the Bibles.

b. A few _____ the mice nibbled my cooking; they must _____ died in agony.

c. John L. Sullivan could _____ won the fight, but he shouldn't _____ trained at any _____ the saloons.

3

a. have, of

b. of, have

c. have, have, of

---

4   hear   here

Copy each phrase twice, including the capital letters.

An EAR can hEAR. _____

_____

HERE and tHERE _____

_____

4

[copy]

5

Write *hear* or *here*.

See my ear? I _____ _____.

5

hear

here

6

Write *hear* or *here*.

a. We'll _____ the wrestlers grunt if we sit _____.

b. That's music? I'd rather _____ a dog fight.

c. _____ ye! _____ ye! _____ comes the king!

6

a. hear, here

b. hear

c. Hear, Hear, Here

---

7   hole   whole

Copy each phrase two times.

bullet hole _____ _____

whole army _____ _____

7

[copy]

8

Write *hole* or *whole*.

I ate the _____ doughnut, including the _____.

---

8 whole hole	**9** Write *hole* or *whole*. a. My glass eye rolled into a gopher _____. b. The _____ truck dropped into a _____. c. Our catcher played the _____ season with a _____ in his pants.

9
 	
a. hole
b. whole,
   hole
c. whole,
   hole
	10 **instance** **instants**
	
	An *instance* is an example.
	Instants are moments.
	
	Copy each phrase two times.
	
	an instance _____ _____
	
	several instants _____ _____

10 [copy]	**11** Write *instance* or *instants*. a. An example (singular) is an _____. b. Fleeting moments (plural) are _____.
11 a. instance b. instants	**12** Write *instance* or *instants*. a. Starving the baby is an _____ of neglect. b. The fifty-yard dash lasts a few _____. c. Our pilot, in one _____, missed a crash by _____.
12 a. instance b. instants c. instance, instants	**13** **knew** **new** Copy each phrase two times. knew him _____ _____ new shoes _____ _____
13 [copy]	**14** Write *knew* or *new*. Hazel soon _____ her _____ schedule.

14 knew new	**15** Write *knew* or *new*. a. She had _____ ideas. That much we _____ . b. Kay _____ that I _____ her _____ plan. c. Try this _____ tool of education: a book.
15 a. new, knew b. knew, knew, new c. new	**16** marital martial *Marital* refers to marriage. *Martial* refers to war (the *ti* has the sound of *sh,* as in *nation*). Pronounce and copy each phrase two times. marital bliss _____ _____ martial law _____ _____
16 [copy]	**17** Write *marital* or *martial*. The captain and his bride led a happy _____ life until the army recalled him to _____ duties.
17 marital martial	**18** Write *marital* or *martial*. a. There's an *sh* sound in *nation* and in _____ . b. The pope said that _____ ties last forever. c. Soldiers march to _____ music, but "I Love You Truly" is _____ music.
18 a. *martial* b. marital c. martial, marital	**19** moral morale *Moral* means "good and honorable"; also, a *moral* is a message. But *morale* (accent on the second syllable) refers to confidence or spirit. Copy each phrase two times. moral conduct _____ _____ army morale _____ _____
19 [copy]	**20** Write *moral* or *morale*. When the team's _____ (spirit) was high, we won games. The _____ (message) is obvious.

20

morale
moral

21

Write *moral* or *morale*.

a. Group spirit is known as _____.

b. Most poems today don't have a _____.

c. Losing forty fights lowered his _____.

d. The _____ of *Pilgrim's Progress* is that a person should lead a _____ life.

21

a. morale
b. moral
c. morale
d. moral,
    moral

---

22   QUIZ

Write in full the words we have studied.

_____ a. Sit [he–].   _____ g. [mor–] code

_____ b. a [–ole] pie   _____ h. I [he–] you.

_____ c. a rare [inst–]   _____ i. team [mora–]

_____ d. [ma–t–l] bliss   _____ j. a [–ew] dress

_____ e. a deep [–ole]   _____ k. [ma–t–l] tanks

_____ f. I [–ew] it!   _____ l. within [inst–]

22

a. here
b. whole
c. instance
d. marital
e. hole
f. knew
g. moral
h. hear
i. morale
j. new
k. martial
l. instants

---

23   of   off

The word *of* ends in a *v* sound.
If you want the *f* sound (*off*, meaning "not on"), be sure to use two *f*'s.

Copy each phrase two times.

one of us   _____

                   _____

He fell off.   _____

                   _____

23

[copy]

24

Write *of* or *off*.

a. The judge looks like one _____ the burglars.

b. The opposite of *on* is _____.

24 a. of b. *off*	**25** Write *of* or *off*. a. One _____ the actors fell _____ the stage. b. We turned _____ the TV set because _____ the commercials. c. Huck Finn took _____ his pants and dived _____ the raft.

25
 	
a. of, off
b. off, of
c. off, off
	26 **pail** **pale**
	
	Copy each phrase two times.
	
	Fill the pail. _____
	
	                      _____
	
	You look pale. _____
	
	                      _____

26 [copy]	**27** Write *pail* or *pale*. Here's a _____ of _____ yellow apples.
27 pail pale	**28** Write *pail* or *pale*. a. Mary read the letter and turned _____. b. Gaston drank _____ wine from a _____. c. The soldier lost a _____ of blood and looked _____.

28
 	
a. pale
b. pale, pail
c. pail, pale
	29 **peace** **piece**
	
	Copy each phrase two times, including the capital letters.
	
	WAR and peACE _____
	
	                      _____
	
	PIEce of PIE _____
	
	                      _____

29 [copy]	**30** a. What vowel in *war* is also in *peace?* _____ b. What letters in *pie* are also in *piece?* _____ c. Let's sign a _____ [p–ce] treaty.

30

a. *a*
b. *pie*
c. peace

31

Write *peace* or *piece*.

a. Stop fighting over a _____ of pie. Let's have _____ around here.

b. Captain Ahab lost a _____ of his ivory leg.

c. Give Pierre his wine, his _____ of bread, his _____ of cheese—and he's at _____ .

31

a. piece
    peace
b. piece
c. piece,
    piece,
    peace

---

32   **personal**   **personnel**

Personal means "private."
Personnel (accent on *nel*) refers to a group of workers.

Copy each phrase two times.

personal habits   _____

                         _____

personnel manager   _____

                         _____

32

[copy]

33

Write *personal* or *personnel*.

The mynah bird made a _____ remark about the _____ of our crew, which I resented.

33

personal
personnel

34

Write *personal* or *personnel*.

a. Apply for a job at the _____ office.

b. Don't use my toothbrush—that's _____ .

c. The foreman fired certain _____ for _____ reasons.

34

a. personnel
b. personal
c. personnel,
   personal

---

35   **principal**   **principle**

Principle refers to a rule or a general truth.
Principal is used for all other meanings and stresses the idea of "main" or "chief."

Copy each phrase two times.

basic principle   _____

                   _____

principal city   _____

                   _____

35

[copy]

36

a. *Principle* means "rule"—and both words end in what two letters? _____

b. Consider the *principal* in a trial or a school or a bank deposit. The word ends in what three letters? _____

36

a. *le*
b. *pal*

37

Write *principal* or *principle*.

a. Dr. Gizmo is our new high school _____.

b. Levers involve a simple _____ (rule).

c. The _____ speaker mumbled about the _____ of effective communication.

d. P. T. Barnum's _____ that "a sucker is born every minute" was a _____ cause of his financial success.

37

a. principal
b. principle
c. principal, principle
d. principle, principal

38   role   roll

Write *role* when you mean a part played, as by an actor. Otherwise, write *roll*.

Copy each phrase twice, including the capital letters.

a stagE rolE _____

_____

roll the ball _____

_____

38

[copy]

39

Write *role* or *roll*.

a. Mr. Snopes ordered coffee and a _____.

b. The word _____, like the word *stage,* ends in an *e.*

39

a. roll
b. *role*

40

Write *role* or *roll*.

a. I'll _____ my eyes in this comic _____.

b. The general read the _____ of fallen heroes; then came a _____ of drums.

c. In his _____ as villain, Rudolph will _____ Daisy off the cliff.

40

a. roll, role
b. roll, roll
c. role, roll

41   **QUIZ**

Write in full the words we have studied.

_____ a. [pa—] of beer

_____ b. jump [—f]

_____ c. comedy [rol—]

_____ d. [p—ce] pact

_____ e. [pa—] lips

_____ f. one [—f] us

_____ g. [rol—] along

_____ h. basic [princ—]

_____ i. [pers—l] favor

_____ j. school [princ—]

_____ k. [pers—] manager

_____ l. [p—ce] of pie

41

a. pail
b. off
c. role
d. peace
e. pale
f. of
g. roll
h. principle
i. personal
j. principal
k. personnel
l. piece

42   **shone**   **shown**

Shone is related to *shine*.
Shown is related to *show*.

Copy each phrase two times.

The sun shone. _____

_____

Films were shown. _____

_____

42

[copy]

43

Write *shone* or *shown*.

a. The past tense of *shine* is _____ .

b. I'll show you tricks never _____ before.

43 a. *shone* b. shown	**44** Write *shone* or *shown*. a. Velma's scars will be _____ to the jury. b. When Captain Kidd was _____ the treasure, his eyes _____. c. The moon _____ over the tombstones as we were _____ the haunted farmhouse.
44 a. shown b. shown, shone c. shone, shown	**45** stake steak Write *steak* if you mean a piece of meat or fish; otherwise, write *stake*. Copy each phrase two times, including the capital letters. wooden stake _____ _____ TEA and STEAK _____ _____
45 [copy]	**46** Write *stake* or *steak*. a. Algernon ordered tea with his _____. b. Joan of Arc was burned at the _____.
46 a. steak b. stake	**47** Write *stake* or *steak*. a. I was served a large but tough _____. b. Edna stumbled over the tent _____. c. Please _____ me to coffee and a _____.
47 a. steak b. stake c. stake, steak	**48** stationary stationery Copy each phrase two times, including the capital letters. STAnd stationAry. _____ _____ StationERY is papER. _____ _____

48

[copy]

49

Write *stationary* or *stationery*.

a. Statues usually stand _____.

b. *Paper* has an *er* in it and so does _____.

49

a. stationary
b. *stationery*

50

Write *stationary* or *stationery*.

a. We sat _____, folding pink _____.

b. The Honda passed me as if I were _____.

c. A _____ sentry held some _____.

50

a. stationary,
   stationery
b. stationary
c. stationary,
   stationery

51　　　　　threw　　　　　through

Copy each phrase two times.

We threw rocks. _____

_____

Run through. _____

_____

51

[copy]

52

Write *threw* or *through*.

a. The past tense of the verb *throw* is _____.

b. Dad saw _____ my alibi and _____ a fit.

52

a. *threw*
b. through,
   threw

53

Write *threw* or *through*.

a. Benny ate five hot dogs, then _____ up.

b. "Scram! You're _____!" shouted my boss, and he _____

   me _____ the door.

53

a. threw
b. through,
   threw,
   through

54　　　　　weak　　　　　week

Copy each phrase two times.

a weak beak _____

_____

busy week _____

_____

---

54 [copy]	**55** Write *weak* or *week*. Dig ditches and you feel _____ at the end of the _____ .
55 weak week	**56** Write *weak* or *week*. a. Shoppers go mad during Christmas _____ . b. Gandhi fasted for a _____ and grew _____ . c. This coffee is so _____ that we'll bury it next _____ .
56 a. week b. week, weak c. weak, week	**57** weather whether Copy each phrase two times. lovely weather _____ _____ whether or not _____ _____
57 [copy]	**58** What are the first two letters of such question words as *why, when, where, what, whither?* _____ Another *wh* word is _____ [–ther].
58 *wh* *whether*	**59** Write *weather* or *whether*. a. Hamlet wondered _____ to be or not to be. b. I love Montana _____ , _____ it stays chilly or climbs way up to twenty below. c. I wonder _____ Alaska has better _____ .

59
 	
a. whether
b. weather,
   whether
c. whether,
   weather
	60 were where
	
	Copy each sentence two times.
	
	We were friends. _____
	
	_____
	
	Where were you? _____
	
	_____

60

[copy]

61

Again—what are the first two letters of *who, why, when, which, whether?*

_____

Another word in this *wh* group is _____ [–ere].

61

wh
where

62

Write *were* or *where.*

a.   Can you see _____ the dog bit me?

b.   You and I _____ young, Maggie.

c.   We _____ here, but _____ _____ you?

62

a. where
b. were
c. were,
     where,
     were

---

63   QUIZ

Write in full the words we have studied.

_____ a. The sun [sh–].

_____ b. white [sta–ry]

_____ c. a six-day [we–k]

_____ d. T-bone [st–]

_____ e. decide [w–th–r] to go

_____ f. Slides were [sho–].

_____ g. [stat–ry] object

_____ h. jumped [thr–] flames

_____ i. rainy [w–th–r]

_____ j. Oh, [w–re] are you?

63

a. shone
b. stationery
c. week
d. steak
e. whether
f. shown
g. stationary
h. through
i. weather
j. where

64

Enter any words that you misspelled in this chapter into your Personal List of Demons in the Appendix.

Fill in the blanks with words studied in this chapter.

1. At the end of the _____ [we–k], God took a day off.

2. Karen studied and she _____ [–ew] the correct spelling.

3. Tattoos covered the sailor's _____ [–ole] body.

4. Now that I can afford a juicy _____ [st–], I have no teeth.

5. Rosa received six birthday gifts of _____ [stat–ry].

6. Thoreau picked a _____ [pa–] of huckleberries.

7. Movies affect our _____ [mora–] standards.

8. Go to church _____ [w–ther] you sinned or not.

9. You must _____ [have/of] been a genius.

10. Bluebeard and his wives needed _____ [ma–t–l] counseling.

11. Army _____ [mora–] was high after the bombing raid.

12. Get your muddy boots _____ [–f] my coffee table.

13. Their _____ [princ–] export is beans.

14. Discover the basic scientific _____ [princip–].

15. The flashlight _____ [sho–] in my eyes.

16. Rudy hugged Sally for a few precious _____ [instan–].

17. Ten below zero was torrid _____ [w–ther] for Eskimos.

18. Apply at the _____ [perso–] office.

19. Olivier played the _____ [ro–] of Hamlet.

20. What do you _____ [he–] from the mob?

21. The president _____ [thr–] the first baseball.

22. Our car began to _____ [rol–] off the cliff.

23. Wanda was _____ [we–k] after her illness.

24. Our _____ [p–ce] treaty swindled the Indians.

25. Tabloid newspapers get fat on _____ [pers–l] gossip.

KEY TO REVIEW TEST

Check your test answers with the following key. Deduct 4% per error from a possible 100%.

1. week	**6.** pail	**11.** morale	**16.** instants	**21.** threw
2. knew	**7.** moral	**12.** off	**17.** weather	**22.** roll
3. whole	**8.** whether	**13.** principal	**18.** personnel	**23.** weak
4. steak	**9.** have	**14.** principle	**19.** role	**24.** peace
5. stationery	**10.** marital	**15.** shone	**20.** hear	**25.** personal

Score: _____ %

SUPPLEMENTARY LIST A

Examine these confusable words carefully, noting the differences in spelling and meaning.

EXERCISE. On a separate piece of paper, use each of the following words in a sentence. Check meaning when necessary in a dictionary. Compare sentences in class.

1. adapt, adopt	**25.** complement, compliment	**49.** meat, meet
2. addition, edition	**26.** costume, custom	**50.** miner, minor
3. alley, ally	**27.** dammed, damned	**51.** naval, navel
4. allowed, aloud	**28.** dear, deer	**52.** peak, peek
5. allusion, illusion	**29.** deceased, diseased	**53.** pedal, petal
6. anecdote, antidote	**30.** dew, do, due	**54.** picture, pitcher
7. ascent, assent	**31.** dyeing, dying	**55.** plain, plane
8. assistance, assistants	**32.** emigrate, immigrate	**56.** pole, poll
9. bare, bear	**33.** eminent, imminent	**57.** pore, pour
10. base, bass	**34.** envelop, envelope	**58.** presence, presents
11. beach, beech	**35.** fair, fare	**59.** profit, prophet
12. beat, beet	**36.** flea, flee	**60.** prophecy, prophesy
13. beside, besides	**37.** flour, flower	**61.** respectfully, respectively
14. board, bored	**38.** foul, fowl	**62.** ring, wring
15. boarder, border	**39.** gild, guild	**63.** road, rode
16. bridal, bridle	**40.** heal, heel	**64.** sail, sale
17. canvas, canvass	**41.** hoarse, horse	**65.** shudder, shutter
18. carton, cartoon	**42.** holey, holy	**66.** steal, steel
19. ceiling, sealing	**43.** huge, Hugh	**67.** straight, strait
20. censor, censure	**44.** incidence, incidents	**68.** summary, summery
21. cereal, serial	**45.** lessen, lesson	**69.** vain, vein
22. chord, cord	**46.** liable, libel	**70.** waist, waste
23. cite, sight, site	**47.** mantel, mantle	
24. coarse, course	**48.** medal, metal	

5

The *Hoping-Hopping* Rule

IN THIS CHAPTER

1. biting	9. fated	17. moped	25. ridding	33. striped
2. bitten	10. fatted	18. mopped	26. riding	34. stripped
3. bitter	11. fibber	19. pining	27. scraped	35. taping
4. coma	12. fiber	20. pinning	28. scrapped	36. tapping
5. comma	13. griping	21. planing	29. shining	37. wining
6. diner	14. gripping	22. planning	30. shinning	38. winning
7. dining	15. hoping	23. raping	31. snipers	39. writing
8. dinner	16. hopping	24. rapping	32. snippers	40. written

COVER THIS COLUMN

1   long vowels   short vowels

Pairs of words, like *writing–written, hoping–hopping, taping–tapping,* won't confuse us if we understand the simple rule behind them.

It's mainly a matter of knowing long vowel sounds and short vowel sounds. Consider the sounds of the vowels—*a, e, i, o, u*—in the following words:

Short vowel sounds: tăp   thĕm   bĭt   hŏp   cŭt   wrĭtten

Long vowel sounds: tāpe   thēme   bīte   hōpe   cūte   wrīting

Write *long* or *short*.

a. The *a* in *rat* and the *i* in *win* have a ——————— vowel sound.

b. The *a* in *rate* and the *i* in *wine* have a ——————— vowel sound.

1 a. short b. long	**2** Fill in the blank. The names of *a, e, i, o, u* have a _____ [long/short] vowel sound.
2 long	**3** Circle the words that have in them a *long* vowel sound. tap hope cut bit tape them bite written theme hop cute writing
3 CIRCLE: bite hope theme tape cute writing	**4** Circle the words that have in them a *long* vowel sound. diner dinner snipers snippers hoping hopping taping tapping planing planning writing written
4 CIRCLE: diner hoping planing snipers taping writing	**5** Fill in the blanks with the right choices. a. **RULE: Long vowel sounds (as in *hōping* and *tāping*) are produced when two vowels are separated by a _____ [single/double] consonant.** b. **RULE: Short vowel sounds (as in *hŏpping* and *tăpping*) are produced when two vowels are separated by a _____ [single/double] consonant.**
5 a. single b. double	**6** writing written Let's apply our rules. a. The first *i* in the word *writ–ng* has a _____ [short/long] vowel sound. Therefore, we put _____ [t/tt] between the vowels, thus: _____ [writ–ng]. b. The *i* in *writ–n* has a _____ [short/long] vowel sound. Therefore, we put _____ [t/tt] between the vowels, thus: _____ [writ–n].

6 a. long 　 t 　 writing b. short 　 tt 　 written	**7** Write the words in full. Bashful Benny began ———————— [writ–g] a love letter, but soon he tore up what he had ———————— [writ–n].
7 writing written	**8**　　　**hoping**　　　**hopping** Copy each phrase two times. hoping to win　　———————————————— 　　　　　　　　　———————————————— hopping on one leg　———————————————— 　　　　　　　　　————————————————
8 [copy]	**9** Write the words in full. Amy is ———————— [hop–g] that her frog Julius wins the ———————— [hop–g] contest.
9 hoping hopping	**10**　　　**taping**　　　**tapping** Copy each phrase two times. taping the torn pages　———————————————— 　　　　　　　　　———————————————— tapping with a hammer　———————————————— 　　　　　　　　　————————————————
10 [copy]	**11** Write the words in full. A raven came ———————— [tap–g] at my chamber door just as I was ———————— [tap–g] a blister on my toe.
11 tapping taping	**12**　　　　　　　　　**QUIZ** Write the words in full. a.　Freddy spent Monday ———————— [writ–ng] an insulting letter to the 　　big fullback and spent Tuesday ———————— [tap–ng] a broken nose.

b. Lulu had _____ [writ–n]: "I'm _____ [hop–ng] mad at you, Freddy, and here's _____ [hop–ng] you never come _____ [tap–ng] at our door again. . . . I'll be home after seven."

12

a. writing,
   taping
b. written,
   hopping,
   hoping,
   tapping

13

Write the words in full.

The trout weren't _____ [bit–ng]; but we were so badly _____ [bit–n] by mosquitoes that my rich uncle became _____ [bit–r] and disinherited me.

13

biting
bitten
bitter

14

Write the words in full.

The passengers ate _____ [din–r] in the _____ [din–r].

14

dinner
diner

15

Write the words in full.

Frank says he can make silk out of wood _____ [fib–r]. What a _____ [fib–r]!

15

fiber
fibber

16

Write the words in full.

Stop your whining and _____ [grip–ng]. Try to enjoy this _____ [grip–ng] three-handkerchief melodrama.

16

griping
gripping

17   **QUIZ**

Write the words in full.

a. When we ate _____ [din–r] in the _____ [din–ng] room, we had jelly on our bread. This made Betty _____ [bit–r] because she likes _____ [but–r] _____ [bet–r].

b. The whale swallowed Jonah without _____ [bit–ng] him, then apparently felt a _____ [grip–ng] from within and spat the indigestible sinner out—a _____ [grip–ng] story!

17
 	
a. dinner,
  dining,
  bitter,
  butter,
  better
b. biting,
  griping,
  gripping
	18
	
	Write the words in full.
	
	The printer left out a _____ [com–]? He must have been in a _____ [com–].

18 comma coma	**19** Write the words in full. The beautiful little pigs were _____ [fat–d] to be _____ [fat–d] and eaten in pork sausages.
19 fated fatted	**20** Write the words in full. Mike reluctantly _____ [mop–d] the floors, then sat in a corner and _____ [mop–d].
20 mopped moped	**21** QUIZ Write the words in full. a. Our slugger, Punchy, was _____ [fat–d] to get a concussion. "He's still in a _____ [com–]," said the doctor. Asked Mary, "How can you tell?" b. The prodigal son got the _____ [fat–d] calf, and the good son _____ [mop–d] because he seemed _____ [fat–d] to get spaghetti without meatballs. c. Oscar Wilde spent a day _____ [mop–ng] up errors in a poem. That whole morning he removed one _____ [com–]. That afternoon he put it in again.

21
 	
a. fated,
  coma
b. fatted,
  moped,
  fated
c. mopping,
  comma
	22
	
	Write the words in full.
	
	Selma is _____ [pin–ng] for the lad who is _____ [pin–ng] his fraternity pin on her sister.

22 pining pinning	**23** Write the words in full. Manuel is _____ [plan–ng] to get married, so he's _____ [plan–ng] boards to build a honeymoon cottage.
23 planning planing	**24** Write the words in full. The judge, after _____ [rap–ng] on the bench with his gavel, sentenced the choir director for _____ [rap–ng] the soprano.
24 rapping raping	**25** QUIZ a. The door was stuck. I tried _____ [rap–ng] it with a hammer and _____ [plan–ng] the edges. Now I'm _____ [plan–ng] to chop it up. b. The district attorney is _____ [pin–ng] charges against Scarface for robbing and _____ [rap–ng] his victims. Soon Scarface will sit in a small cell, _____ [pin–ng] for liberty and _____ [plan–ng] a few more nasty crimes.

25
 	
a. rapping,
  planing,
  planning
b. pinning,
  raping,
  pining,
  planning
	26
	
	Write the words in full.
	
	Jason went _____ [rid–ng] to the gambling dens in a small cheap car and came back _____ [rid–ng] a big expensive one—the bus. That's what _____ [rid–ng] yourself of money will do.

26 riding riding ridding	**27** Write the words in full. Who _____ [scrap–d] the fender of the new Buick? Mr. and Mrs. Fuddle _____ [scrap–d] about that last night.
27 scraped scrapped	**28** Write the words in full. Her eyes _____ [shin–ng], little Helen began _____ [shin–ng] up the apple tree.

28 shining shinning	**29** **QUIZ** Write the words in full. a. All morning my shovel _____ [scrap–d] the sidewalk, _____ [rid–ng] it of snow. Then out came the _____ [shin–ng] sun and melted everything. b. The Human Fly started _____ [shin–ng] up the wall of the sky-scraper, but he _____ [scrap–d] the plan when the sheriff came _____ [rid–ng] up and pointed a gun at him.

29
 	
a. scraped,
    ridding,
    shining
b. shinning,
    scrapped,
    riding
	30
	
	Write the words in full.
	
	In the jungle, Percy had only a pair of steel _____ [snip–rs] to defend himself against _____ [snip–rs].

30 snippers snipers	**31** Write the words in full. Sam studied spelling all evening (a splendid habit); then he _____ [strip–d] to the skin and put on his _____ [strip–d] pajamas.
31 stripped striped	**32** Write the words in full. After _____ [win–ng] the World Series, the Dodger players did a bit of fancy _____ [win–ng] and _____ [din–ng].
32 winning wining dining	**33** **QUIZ** Write the words in full. a. I tried to chase the smelly _____ [strip–d] skunks with my garden _____ [snip–rs], but the little _____ [snip–rs] used live ammunition and had no trouble _____ [win–ng] the argument. b. Sergeant Belcher did too much _____ [win–ng] and boozing; so he was _____ [strip–d] of his rank.

33

a. striped,
   snippers,
   snipers,
   winning
b. wining,
   stripped

34

Enter any words that you misspelled in this chapter into your Personal List of Demons in the Appendix.

Fill in the blanks with words studied in this chapter.

1. A girl with a _____ [win–ng] smile

2. A candle _____ [shin–ng] in the darkness

3. _____ [rid–ng] on a bad-tempered horse

4. _____ [pin–ng] his pants to his shirt

5. Knuckles _____ [rap–ng] on the door

6. Proper use of semicolon and _____ [c–ma]

7. Lincoln, a man _____ [fat–d] to be president.

8. Idiots _____ [hop–ng] to win the lottery.

9. Cloth from genuine cotton _____ [fib–r]

10. A frosty and _____ [bit–ng] north wind

11. _____ [mop–d] and polished the floors

12. Torn pages that need _____ [tap–ng]

13. Trimming the hedge with _____ [snip–rs]

14. Great poems yet to be _____ [writ–n]

15. A frog _____ [hop–ng] into the swamp

16. Devouring a turkey _____ [din–r]

17. Pills with a _____ [bit–r] taste

18. Spoons that _____ [scrap–d] the dessert dish

19. _____ [tap–ng] a rhythm on bongo drums

20. A jungle guarded by _____ [snip–rs]

21. A zebra, like a _____ [strip–d] horse

22. _____ [writ–ng] a fat novel

23. Bean soup in the _____ [din–ng] room

24. _____ [grip–ng] the drowning man by the hair

25. Prisoners _____ [plan–ng] to escape

KEY TO REVIEW TEST

Check your test answers with the following key. Deduct 4% per error from a possible 100%.

1. winning	**6.** comma	**11.** mopped	**16.** dinner	**21.** striped
2. shining	**7.** fated	**12.** taping	**17.** bitter	**22.** writing
3. riding	**8.** hoping	**13.** snippers	**18.** scraped	**23.** dining
4. pinning	**9.** fiber	**14.** written	**19.** tapping	**24.** gripping
5. rapping	**10.** biting	**15.** hopping	**20.** snipers	**25.** planning

Score: _____%

6

Fight Those Demons! (1–35)

IN THIS CHAPTER

1. a lot
2. absence
3. across
4. actually
5. afraid
6. again
7. all right

8. allowed
9. almost
10. although
11. always
12. amateur
13. among
14. amount

15. analyze
16. angry
17. anxious
18. apparently
19. argument
20. article
21. athlete

22. aunt
23. awful
24. awkward
25. bachelor
26. bargain
27. barrel
28. beautiful

29. benefit
30. bicycle
31. building
32. business
33. candidate
34. cemetery
35. convenient

COVER THIS COLUMN

1			
a lot	**absence**	**across**	**actually**
afraid	**again**	**all right**	

Copy each demon two times, first in print, then in handwriting. Memorize as you write.

	Print	Handwriting
a lot	_____	_____
absence	_____	_____
across	_____	_____
actually	_____	_____
afraid	_____	_____
again	_____	_____
all right	_____	_____

1 [copy]	**2** a. The opposite of *all wrong* is _____ . b. The opposite of *a little* is _____ . c. How many *c*'s in *across?* _____ How many *f*'s in *afraid?* _____ (Always check such details.)
2 a. *all right* b. *a lot* c. one one	**3** Write the words in full. (Note that the hyphens do *not* necessarily mean that a letter has been left out.) During your _____ [a–b–s–n–e] I was _____ [a–c–t–l–y] _____ [–f–r–a–d–] I wouldn't ever see you _____ [a–g–n]. I missed you _____ [–l–o–t]. Yes, I almost felt like walking _____ [a–c–r–s–] the street to the hospital to see if you were _____ [a–l–r–i–t–].
3 absence actually afraid again a lot across all right	**4** Write the words in full. Dear Jason: I wore your necktie _____ [a–g–n] during your _____ [a–b–s–n–]. It fell into the soup when I leaned _____ [a–c–r–s–] the table, and I'm _____ [a–f–r–d–] the stains didn't _____ [a–c–t–l–y] improve the tie _____ [a–l–o–t]. I hope it's _____ [a–l–r–i–t–] with you.
4 again absence across afraid actually a lot all right	**5** PROOFREADING. Cross out any misspelled words below and write the correct spelling above them. After an absense of two weeks, Mr. Schultz drove across town again to his dentist and complained: "I'm afrade these false teeth don't fit. I like them a lot, but they don't actually fit."—The dentist checked and said: "They fit your mouth alright."—Mr. Schultz answered: "The glass! At night they don't fit into the glass."

5

absence
afraid
all right

6   allowed   almost   although   always
         amateur   among   amount

Copy each demon two times, first in print, then in handwriting. Memorize as you write.

	Print	Handwriting
allowed		
almost		
although		
always		
amateur		
among		
amount		

6

[copy]

7

Write the words in full.

_____ [A–l–t–h–o–] the forecast was "sunny," we were _____ [a–l–m–s–t] drowned by a record _____ [a–m–n–t] of rain. I waded in the soggy park _____ [a–m–n–g–] the other _____ [a–m–t–r–] gardeners. As _____ [a–l–w–s–], the sign said, "No dogs _____ [a–l–w–d]," but my dog can't read.

7

Although
almost
amount
among
amateur
always
allowed

8

Write the words in full.

A boy who is _____ [a–l–o–d] to grow up _____ [a–m–n–g–] gangs won't _____ [a–m–n–t] to much. But Elmer, from a family of _____ [a–m–t–r–] athletes, has _____ [a–m–s–t–] _____ [a–l–w–y–s] had worthy goals. He was shaped by his grandmother, who still runs marathons _____ , [a–l–t–h–o–] she's eighty.

8

allowed
among
amount
amateur
almost
always
although

9

PROOFREADING. Cross out any misspelled words and write the correct spelling above them.

Although Melvin was an amature boxer, he was allowed a small amount of money because he broke his nose. Melvin learned that if you lie down amoung dogs, you almost all ways get up with fleas.

9

amateur
among
always

10   analyze   angry   anxious   apparently
argument   article   athlete

Copy each demon two times, first in print, then in handwriting. Memorize as you write.

	Print	Handwriting
analyze	_____	_____
angry	_____	_____
anxious	_____	_____
apparently	_____	_____
argument	_____	_____
article	_____	_____
athlete	_____	_____

10

[copy]

11

Write the words in full.

At the zoo our star _____ [a–t–h–l–t–] was _____ [a–p–r–n–t–l–y] having a brotherly _____ [a–r–g–m–n–t] with an _____ [–n–g–r–y] gorilla. Our football coach is _____ [a–n–x–s–] to _____ [a–n–l–z–e] the cause of that dispute, according to a sports _____ [a–r–t–c–l–].

11

athlete
apparently
argument
angry
anxious
analyze
article

12

Write the words in full.

I don't like _____ [–r–g–m–n–t], but a recent sports _____ [a–r–t–c–l–] made me _____ [–n–g–r–y]. The writer _____ [–p–r–n–t–l–y] brags that an ignorant _____ [a–t–l–e–t–] can earn twenty times as much as a skilled surgeon. Now I'm _____ [–n–x–u–s–] to _____ [–n–l–z–] the reasons for the salary difference.

12

argument
article
angry
apparently
athlete
anxious
analyze

13

PROOFREADING. Cross out any misspelled words and write the correct spelling above them.

Our baseball coach, after an angery argument, was apparently amazed when one weak athalete actualy got a base hit. The coach grabbed the ball: "I'm anxious to analyze this round artical for drugs."

13

angry
athlete
actually
article

14

	aunt	awful	awkward	bachelor
	bargain	barrel	beautiful	

Copy each demon two times, first in print, then in handwriting. Memorize as you write.

	Print	Handwriting
aunt	_____	_____
awful	_____	_____
awkward	_____	_____
bachelor	_____	_____
bargain	_____	_____
barrel	_____	_____
beautiful	_____	_____

14

[copy]

15

Write the words in full.

My _____ [a–n–t–] said the pickles were _____ [b–u–t–f–l–] and a real _____ [b–r–g–n–] at two dollars a _____ [b–a–r–l–]. "But they taste _____ [a–f–l–]," said the _____ [b–a–c–h–l–r–]. Then came an _____ [–a–k–w–r–d–] silence.

15

aunt
beautiful
bargain
barrel
awful
bachelor
awkward

16

Write the words in full.

"Your _____ [a–n–t–] is _____ [–a–f–l–] _____ [b–u–t–f–l–]," confided the _____ [b–a–c–h–l–r–]. "I know I'm _____ [–a–k–w–r–d–] and I'm no _____ [b–r–g–n–] or I'd give her a _____ [b–a–r–l–] of kisses."

16

aunt
awful
beautiful
bachelor
awkward
bargain
barrel

17

PROOFREADING. Cross out any misspelled words and write the correct spelling above them.

"It's true," said my ant, "that the bachler is pretty awkward and he's no great bargin; but he does say beautiful things and what would be so aweful if he gave me a barrel of kisses?"

17

aunt
bachelor
bargain
awful

18

	benefit	bicycle	building	business
	candidate	cemetery	convenient	

Copy each demon two times, first in print, then in handwriting. Memorize as you write.

	Print	Handwriting
benefit	_____	_____
bicycle	_____	_____
building	_____	_____
business	_____	_____
candidate	_____	_____
cemetery	_____	_____
convenient	_____	_____

18

[copy]

19

Write the words in full.

I decided to ride a _____ [b–i–c–c–l–] to _____ [b–e–n–f–t–] my health. The result was that I nearly became a _____ [c–a–n–d–a–t–] for a home in the _____ [c–e–m–t–r–y]. A burglar stopped my bike behind a _____ [b–i–l–d–n–g]. "P-please put that p-pistol away," I said, "if it's _____ [c–o–n–v–e–n–t] with you." Replied the stranger, "Don't tell me how to run my _____ [b–s–n–e–s–]."

19

bicycle
benefit
candidate
cemetery
building
convenient
business

20

Write the words in full.

Mr. Sneed opened his banking _____ [b–s–n–e–s] in a small _____ [b–i–l–d–g] near the town _____ [c–e–m–t–r–y]. "My bank," he said, "is for the _____ [b–e–n–f–t–] of those who want their last resting place to be _____ [c–o–n–v–n–t] to their money." Mr. Sneed is now a _____ [c–a–n–d–a–t–e] for mayor, and he rides around town on a _____ [b–c–c–l–] soliciting votes.

20

business
building
cemetery
benefit
convenient
candidate
bicycle

21

PROOFREADING. Cross out any misspelled words and write the correct spelling above them.

A sad-looking man got off his bicycle and parked it next to the bilding. He kneeled at the cemetary grave and sobbed, "Why did you die? Why did you die?" A stranger spoke softly to him, "I'm a canidate for sheriff. It's none of my business but you must truly have loved your wife. For my benefit, tell me about this wonderful woman, if it's convenient." The grieving man answered, "This is the grave of my wife's first husband."

21

building
cemetery
candidate

22

Enter any words that you misspelled in this chapter into your Personal List of Demons in the Appendix.

REVIEW TEST: CHAPTER 6

Fill in the blanks with words studied in this chapter.

1. I never stop to debate with an _____ [a–g–r–y] bull.

2. Even the grass was dead in our _____ [c–e–m–t–r–y].

3. When you're starving, potatoes look _____ [b–u–t–f–l].

4. Our president earns less than an _____ [a–t–l–e–t–e].

5. Only an idiot walks _____ [a–c–r–o–s–] a freeway.

6. Our pilot and copilot were _____ [a–c–t–u–l–y] sober.

7. After a meal the _____ [b–a–c–h–l–r] washed his dish.

8. Who's _____ [a–f–r–a–d–] of the big bad wolf?

9. The farmers sat around a _____ [b–a–r–l–] of pickles.

10. My suit was a _____ [b–a–r–g–n–]—and looked like it.

11. For health and economy, ride a _____ [b–i–c–l–e–].

12. Only Einstein could _____ [a–n–l–z–e–] this problem.

13. When flat on our back, we _____ [a–l–w–a–s] look up.

14. Zha Zha's wedding was no _____ [a–m–t–r–] performance.

15. The firemen had a heated _____ [a–r–g–m–n–t].

16. Ike's eyes bulged as he read the news _____ [a–r–t–c–l–].

17. Money can be very _____ [c–n–v–e–n–i–t].

18. Junior _____ [a–p–r–n–t–l–y] bit the dentist's finger.

19. The sermon on sin was for our special _____ [b–e–n–f–t–].

20. A one-eyed man is king _____ [a–m–n–g–] the blind.

21. After the wedding we picked up _____ [a–l–o–t–] of rice.

22. How's _____ [b–s–n–e–s–]?

23. Mr. Dingle is a promising _____ [c–a–n–d–a–t–e].

24. Smoking is not _____ [a–l–o–d] in this theater.

25. Kulak had warm thoughts, _____ [a–l–t–h–o–] it was forty below.

KEY TO REVIEW TEST

Check your answers with the following key. Deduct 4% per error from a possible 100%.

1. angry	**6.** actually	**11.** bicycle	**16.** article	**21.** a lot
2. cemetery	**7.** bachelor	**12.** analyze	**17.** convenient	**22.** business
3. beautiful	**8.** afraid	**13.** always	**18.** apparently	**23.** candidate
4. athlete	**9.** barrel	**14.** amateur	**19.** benefit	**24.** allowed
5. across	**10.** bargain	**15.** argument	**20.** among	**25.** although

Score: _____%

7

Word Building

IN THIS CHAPTER

COVER THIS COLUMN

1   prefix   suffix

Sometimes we can spell a long word by adding prefixes and suffixes to a short word.

Common prefixes (letters added to the *front* of words): an, ante, anti, com, con, contra, de, dis, ex, extra, il, im, in, inter, ir, mis, over, pre, pro, re, retro, semi, sub, super, trans, un, under

Common suffixes (letters added to the *end* of words): able, al, ally, ance, ant, ar, ary, ate, dom, ence, ent, er, ery, ess, ible, ing, ism, ly, ment, or, ory, sion, tion, ty, y

Write *prefix* or *suffix:*

a. semi _____ c. ery _____

b. ism _____ d. dis _____

1

a. prefix
b. suffix
c. suffix
d. prefix

2 **misunderstanding**

Suppose you feel shaky about a long word, like *misunderstanding*. Build the word. Think of the root *stand;* then add prefixes, suffixes, and word parts.

a. mis + under + stand + ing = _____

b. The skunk and I had a little _____ [m–d–rst–d–ng].

2

a. misunderstanding
b. misunderstanding

3 **superintendent**

The man or woman who runs a school system has a big title. But think of the root *tend;* then add the trimmings.

a. super + in + tend + ent = _____

b. Mr. Fuddle was _____ [s–p–t] of schools.

3

a. superintendent
b. superintendent

4 **internationalism**

Think of *nation*—then add the trimmings.

a. inter + nation + al + ism = _____

b. Cooperation among nations is _____ [i–n–m].

4

a. internationalism
b. internationalism

5 **subatomic**

Think of *atom*. Then add the trimmings.

a. sub + atom + ic = _____

b. An electron is a _____ [s–b–t–c] particle.

5

a. subatomic
b. subatomic

6 **QUIZ**

Write the words in full.

a. The League of Nations ended all war—or tried to—by providing countries with a friendly _____ [i–t–na–l–sm].

b. The doctor made me strip naked. But I was delivering a telegram. What a _____ [m–und–st–d–ng]!

c. School salaries—from _____ [s–p–ten–t] to beginning teacher—were often tiny, almost _____ [s–b–t–c].

6	7 discovery recovering
a. internationalism b. misunderstanding c. superintendent, subatomic	Make up and spell two longer words by adding prefixes or suffixes to each word at the left. Use your dictionary if necessary. cover _discovery_ _recovering_ diction _____ _____ port _____ _____
7 EXAMPLES: prediction dictionary contradiction deport important portable	**8** Continue as in frame 7. govern _____ _____ real _____ _____ natural _____ _____
8 EXAMPLES: government governor misgovern unreal really realism supernatural naturalism naturally	**9** Continue as in frame 7. hero _____ _____ safe _____ _____ state _____ _____ (Compare your word-building creations with those of other students.)
9 EXAMPLES: heroic heroism antihero safety safely unsafe interstate stately misstatement	**10** **RULE: A long word is usually made up of smaller words and pieces, and it is easier to spell the long word if you sound it out and spell it _____ [all/a small piece] at a time.** For instance, the extremely long and rather useless *antidisestablishmentarianism* is quite easy to spell if you sound it out a small piece at a time, something like this: *an ti dis es tab lish men tar i an ism*. No, this old freight train of a word will not be included in any of your spelling tests. We need the space for more important words.

10 a small piece	**11** disagree disappoint dissimilar disappear dissatisfy dissolve Look at the *s*'s in the following combinations. dis + similar = dissimilar dis + appear = disappear a. **RULE: When a prefix like *dis* that ends in an *s* is put in front of a word like *similar* that begins with an *s*, the result is *dissimilar*, which has a total of _____*s*'s.** b. **RULE: When a prefix like *dis* that ends in an *s* is put in front of a word like *appear* that does not begin with an *s*, the result is *disappear*, which has a total of _____*s*'s.**
11 a. two b. one	**12** Write each combination word two times. dis + agree = *disagree* *disagree* dis + appear = _____ _____ dis + appoint = _____ _____ dis + satisfy = _____ _____ dis + similar = _____ _____ dis + solve = _____ _____
12 disappear disappoint dissatisfy dissimilar dissolve	**13** Write in full the combination word that begins with *dis*. a. He sold me a bridge, then _____ [–appeared]. b. Boys and girls are _____ [–similar], a happy arrangement. c. The firemen had a heated _____ [–cussion].
13 a. disappeared b. dissimilar c. discussion	**14** Continue as in frame 13. a. The baseball umpire's lunch _____ [–agreed] with him. b. Pappy _____ [–solves] sugar cubes between his gums. c. Aim high, and you may be _____ [–appointed]. d. If _____ [–satisfied], see our manager. He's in Europe.

14	15	QUIZ

14

a. disagreed
b. dissolves
c. disappointed
d. dissatisfied

15 QUIZ

Write the words in full.

Our caskets now on sale will not _____ [dis–p–nt] or _____ [dis–t–fy] you. They are all _____ [dis–m–l–r] in design and made of materials that will not _____ [dis–lve]. You cannot _____ [dis–gree]—these bargain caskets will _____ [dis–pear] fast.

15

disappoint
dissatisfy
dissimilar
dissolve
disagree
disappear

16

Let's see if the rule for *dis* combinations also applies to other prefixes.

im + perfect = imperfect
im + *m*oral = *imm*oral

mis + taken = mistaken
mi*s* + *s*pell = mi*ss*pell

un + common = uncommon
u*n* + *n*ecessary = u*nn*ecessary

RULE OF ADDITIVE DOUBLING: When the last letter of a prefix is the same as the first letter of the root, we _____ [do/don't] have additive doubling (a doubling of letters).

16

do

17

Apply the rule of additive doubling.
Write each combination two times.

mis+ fortune = _____   _____

im + mature = _____   _____

un + lucky = _____   _____

mis+ step = _____   _____

17

misfortune
immature
unlucky
misstep

18

Write each combination two times.

im + modest = _____   _____

mis+ judge = _____   _____

ir + regular = _____   _____

pre + eminent = _____   _____

18 immodest misjudge irregular preeminent	**19** Write the words in full. (Watch out for hyphens where no letters may be missing.) If I'm not _____ [m–i–s–taken], Bill was an _____ [i–m–a–ture] student with _____ [i–m–perfect] attendance; and though he was a shear leader at Barber College, it was his _____ [m–i–s–f–ortune] to be dropped for cutting classes.
19 mistaken immature imperfect misfortune	**20** Continue as in frame 19. This may seem _____ [i–r–e–gul–r], or at least _____ [u–n–com–on], but I was _____ [u–n–lucky] enough to own a car so old that its license plates were in Roman numerals.
20 irregular uncommon unlucky	**21** Continue as in frame 19. Swimsuits that Grandma would call _____ [i–m–o–dest], if not _____ [i–m–or–l], are now cut out with tiny scissors by _____ [pr–e–min–nt] designers.
21 immodest immoral preeminent	**22** Continue as in frame 19. How _____ [u–n–e–c–s–r–y] it is to _____ [m–i–s–pe–l] when you can now use a clever invention known as a dictionary. Pretend that each _____ [m–i–s–tep] will cost you a fingernail, and you won't _____ [m–i–s–j–dge] another word.
22 unnecessary misspell misstep misjudge	**23** Write *a* or *b* in the parentheses. Additive doubling takes place when the last letter of the prefix and the first letter of the root word are (a) the same, (b) different. ( ) Additive doubling will take place if the prefix *im* is added to the root word (a) *patient,* (b) *material.* ( )

23 (a) (b)	**24** QUIZ Write the words in full. Any cursing at _____ [m–i–s–fort–n–] is _____ [u–n–ec–s–ry], _____ [i–m–ature], and _____ [i–m–or–l]. It is a sign, if I am not _____ [m–i–s–taken], of _____ [i–m–p–rfect] character. Still, an _____ [i–m–odest] oath—please don't _____ [m–i–s–ju–ge] me—often affords me _____ [u–n–com–n] relief.
24 misfortune unnecessary immature immoral mistaken imperfect immodest misjudge uncommon	**25** **RULE: Additive doubling usually applies to combinations of words, word parts, and suffixes.** Write each combination two times. book + keeper = _____ _____ drunken + ness = _____ _____ extra + ordinary = _____ _____ may + be = _____ _____ room + mate = _____ _____ with + hold = _____ _____

25
 	
bookkeeper
drunkenness
extraordinary
maybe
roommate
withhold
	26
	
	Write the combinations in full.
	
	a. Ishmael didn't want the cannibal as his _____ [ro–mate].
	
	b. If lawmakers _____ [wi–hold] more income tax, my salary
	     will _____ [dis–pe–r].
	
	c. My _____ [ro–mate] said I had an _____
	     [extr–dinary] singing voice, but he would stay with me anyhow.

26
 	
a. roommate
b. withhold,
    disappear
c. roommate,
    extraordinary
	27
	
	Write the combinations in full.
	
	a. The _____ [bo–keeper] who fled was five feet tall and fifty
	     thousand dollars short.
	
	b. E.A. Poe, an angel and a glorious wretch, died in _____
	     [drunken–ss].
	
	c. There's a fly in my soup, but _____ [ma–b–] I need the protein.

27 a. bookkeeper b. drunkenness c. maybe	**28** QUIZ Our _____ [book–eper] was fired for _____ [extra–ry] bouts of _____ [drunken–ss]. But _____ [ma–b–] he'll be rehired if his _____ [room–te] can _____ [with–ld] the bottle from him.
28 bookkeeper extraordinary drunkenness maybe roommate withhold	**29** EXCEPTIONS **Please note:** come + ing = coming use + ing = using love + able = lovable Fill in the blank with the correct choice. Words like *come, use,* and *love* that end in *e* _____ [drop/don't drop] that *e* when a suffix is added that begins with a vowel. This subject will be discussed in chapter 9, "Final Silent *e*."
29 drop	**30** Enter any words that you misspelled in this chapter into your Personal List of Demons in the Appendix.

Fill in the blanks with words studied in this chapter.

1. Never _____ [dis–gree] with a teacher before finals.

2. Everything you like is illegal, _____ [im–ral], or fattening.

3. My boss fines me a dollar for every word that I _____ [m–spell].

4. A computer? Our _____ [book–eper] still uses a feather pen.

5. Woodrow Wilson dreamt of a world federation—_____ [int–nat–n–ism].

6. An electron is a _____ [s–b–tom–c] particle.

7. I followed the monkey act and people _____ [re–ly] thought it was an encore.

8. As a schoolboy, the convict had majored in hookey—that was his first _____ [mi–step].

9. Meals for the homeless are scanty and _____ [ir–gular].

10. Two rich fleas bought a dog. They weren't _____ [dis–pointed].

11. The band is playing, or _____ [ma–b–] just tuning up.

12. Bob was young once but is _____ [im–ture] forever.

13. My magic act made the audience _____ [dis–pear].

14. The suppression of women was a stupid _____ [mi–fort–ne].

15. The undertaker wrote "Eventually yours," and that seemed _____ [un–ces–ry].

16. The tax collectors plan to _____ [wi–hold] enough of my salary to build another battleship.

17. _____ [Drunken–ss] on the highway is murder.

18. The teacher with a better car than the _____ [sup–r–tend–nt] was not rehired.

19. Dora bought a _____ [port–bl–] TV set but couldn't lift it.

20. If Moses had been _____ [us–ng] Nixon's secretary, we'd have only eight commandments.

21. A jogger's legs should be long enough, _____ [nat–r–ly], to reach the ground.

22. Joe looks like Shakespeare, but the brains are _____ [d–simil–r].

23. My flat-nosed friend was once a _____ [p–eminent] pugilist.

24. In TV commercials these aspirins _____ [dis–lve] in two seconds.

25. My _____ [ro–mate] is too cowardly to fight and too fat to run.

KEY TO REVIEW TEST

Check your test answers with the following key. Deduct 4% per error from a possible 100%.

1. disagree
2. immoral
3. misspell
4. bookkeeper
5. internation-
   alism
6. subatomic
7. really
8. misstep
9. irregular
10. disappointed
11. maybe
12. immature
13. disappear
14. misfortune
15. unnecessary
16. withhold
17. Drunkenness
18. superinten-
    dent
19. portable
20. using
21. naturally
22. dissimilar
23. preeminent
24. dissolve
25. roommate

Score: _____%

8

Noun Plurals

IN THIS CHAPTER

1   desks   ideas   boxes

Let's see how we usually form the plurals of nouns.

Add *s*.	Add *es*.
desk, desks	box, boxes
slum, slums	church, churches
noodle, noodles	glass, glasses
pencil, pencils	dish, dishes
idea, ideas	walrus, walruses

a. Most nouns—such as *desk, slum,* and *noodle*—become plural when we simply add the letter _____ .

b. Nouns like *box, church,* and *glass* that end in a hissing sound (*s, x, z, ch, sh*) would be _____ [easy/hard] to pronounce if we added only an *s.* So we have to add the letters _____ .

1

a. *s*
b. hard, *es*

2

a. Circle the words that end in a hissing sound.

boy   building   girl   rat

bullet   crash   mess   watch

b. These circled words become plural when we add _____ .

2

a. CIRCLE:
    crash
    mess
    watch
b. *es*

3

RULE: To form plurals, most singular nouns add _____ , but singular nouns that end with a hissing sound add _____ .

3

s
es

4

In fact, if we have to pronounce an extra syllable in the plural (example: *box, boxes; church, churches*), it usually means that the letters _____ have been added.

4

es

5

Write the plurals.

shepherd, *shepherds*   tax, _____

boss, *bosses*   business, _____

stitch, _____   pamphlet, _____

argument, _____   vacuum, _____

5 stitches arguments taxes businesses pamphlets vacuums	**6** Continue as in frame 5. description, _____ lash, _____ crutch, _____ princess, _____ radio, _____ schedule, _____ roommate, _____ arch, _____
6 descriptions crutches radios roommates lashes princesses schedules arches	**7** Write the plurals. a. Dazzy could sell _____ [comb–] and _____ [brush–] to a bald man. b. He called us a pack of _____ [fool–] and _____ [wretch–]. c. The queen wore _____ [topaz–] and _____ [pearl–].

7
 	
a. combs,
    brushes
b. fools,
    wretches
c. topazes,
    pearls
	8 **turkeys** **enemies**
	
	Let's see how we form the plurals of nouns that end in *y*.
	
	      Add *s*. Change *y* to *i* and add *es*.
	   turkey, turkeys navy, navies
	   boy, boys enemy, enemies
	   tray, trays family, families
	
	a. When a singular noun has a vowel in front of the final *y* (as in *turkey, boy, tray*), we form the plural by adding _____ .
	
	b. When a singular noun has a consonant in front of the final *y* (as in *navy, enemy, family*), we change the *y* to *i* and add _____ .

8 a. *s* b. *es*	**9** **RULE: A noun like *turkey* that ends in *y* with a _____ [v–] in front of it adds _____ to form the plural *turkeys*; a noun like *navy* that ends in *y* with a _____ [con–] in front of it changes its *y* to *i* and adds _____ .**
9 vowel *s* consonant *es*	**10** Write the plurals. a. donkey, _donkeys_ d. story, _____ b. city, _cities_ e. valley, _____ c. dray, _____ f. alley, _____

10

c. drays
d. stories
e. valleys
f. alleys

11

Write the plurals.

a. luxury, _____
b. cemetery, _____
c. toy, _____

d. baby, _____
e. army, _____
f. subway, _____

11

a. luxuries
b. cemeteries
c. toys
d. babies
e. armies
f. subways

12

Write the plurals.

a. volley, _____
b. category, _____
c. tragedy, _____

d. boundary, _____
e. library, _____
f. journey, _____

12

a. volleys
b. categories
c. tragedies
d. boundaries
e. libraries
f. journeys

13   **Kennedys**

EXCEPTION: **Note that proper nouns (names) are an exception to the rule.**

Study the example:

The Kennedys and the Clancys were at the wake.

Both *Kennedy* and *Clancy* end in *y* with a consonant in front of it, but **the name is kept intact,** and we form the plural simply by adding the letter

_____ .

13

s

14

Write the plurals.

a. McCurdy, *McCurdys*   c. Germany, _____
b. July, _____   d. Mary, _____

14

b. Julys
c. Germanys
d. Marys

15   **QUIZ**

Write the plurals.

a. Freud had a few amazing _____ [theory].
b. Here clashed two mighty _____ [army].
c. We had two _____ [Henry] in our class.
d. Sally is torn by many _____ [jealousy].

e. The explorer saw many fertile _____ [valley] and queenly _____ [lady].

f. Take _____ [donkey] around the world and you'll still have _____ [donkey].

15

a. theories
b. armies
c. Henrys
d. jealousies
e. valleys, ladies
f. donkeys, donkeys

16   altos   radios   photos

Most nouns that end in *o* follow the basic rule—that is, they add *s* to form the plural.

Study the examples:

  MUSICAL TERMS: altos, banjos, concertos, contraltos, piccolos, sopranos

  WORDS WITH A VOWEL BEFORE THE FINAL *O*: cameos, curios, folios, igloos, patios, radios, scenarios

  MISCELLANEOUS: dynamos, Eskimos, ghettos, lassos, mementos, photos, silos, tobaccos

Adding *s,* write the plural three times.

solo   _____   _____   _____

patio   _____   _____   _____

ghetto _____   _____   _____

16

solos
patios
ghettos

17

Since *piano* is a musical term, we know that we form its plural by adding the letter _____. The result is _____.

17

s
pianos

18

Since *studio* has a vowel before the final *o,* we know that we form its plural by adding the letter _____. The result is _____.

18

s
studios

19   potatoes   echoes   heroes

EXCEPTIONS: Ten nouns, however, that end in *o* must add *es* to form the plural. Study them carefully. In alphabetic order they are *buffalo, echo, embargo, hero, Negro, no, potato, tomato, torpedo, veto.*

Write the plurals of these exceptions that require an *es.*

buffalo, ___*buffaloes*___   no, _____

echo, ___*echoes*___   potato, _____

embargo, _____   tomato, _____

hero, _____   torpedo, _____

Negro, _____   veto, _____

19	20	QUIZ

19

embargoes
heroes
Negroes
noes
potatoes
tomatoes
torpedoes
vetoes

20

Write the plurals of these nouns that end in *o*. (HINT: Add *s,* unless the word is one of the ten exceptions listed in frame 19.)

solo, _____*solos*_____   tomato, _____

torpedo, _____*torpedoes*_____   portfolio, _____

rodeo, _____   embargo, _____

ego, _____   allegro, _____

20

rodeos
egos
tomatoes
portfolios
embargoes
allegros

21

Continue as in frame 20.

zero, _____   veto, _____

soprano, _____   embryo, _____

ratio, _____   buffalo, _____

21

zeros
sopranos
ratios
vetoes
embryos
buffaloes

22

Continue as in frame 20.

cello, _____   vibrato, _____

potato, _____   hero, _____

Negro, _____   trio, _____

22

cellos
potatoes
Negroes
vibratos
heroes
trios

23   **beliefs**   **selves**

Most nouns that end in *f* follow the basic rule—that is, they add *s* to form the plural.

Study the examples:
    beliefs, briefs, chefs, chiefs, griefs, gulfs, oafs, reefs, reproofs, serfs, waifs

Some nouns, however, that end in *f* or *fe* have plurals ending in *ves*.

Study this *ves* group carefully. Pronounce the plurals correctly several times as you fill in the blanks.

calf, _____*calves*_____   loaf, _____

elf, _____*elves*_____   self, _____

half, _____   shelf, _____

knife, _____   thief, _____

leaf, _____   wife, _____

life, _____   wolf, _____

23	24

23

halves
knives
leaves
lives
loaves
selves
shelves
thieves
wives
wolves

24

Write the plurals of these nouns ending in *f*. Add *s* or switch to the *ves* ending as necessary.

shelf, _____ *shelves*   chef, _____

gulf, _____ *gulfs*   wolf, _____

belief, _____   reef, _____

wife, _____   self, _____

leaf, _____   life, _____

brief, _____   thief, _____

24

beliefs
wives
leaves
briefs
chefs
wolves
reefs
selves
lives
thieves

25   **QUIZ**

Write the correct plural forms.

a. Rake up all the fallen _____ [leaf].

b. I can't share your crazy _____ [belief].

c. Buy me three crusty _____ [loaf].

d. The sultan had seven _____ [wife].

e. Between us are wide _____ [gulf].

f. Girls! Look out for _____ [yoursel–].

g. We must look out for _____ [oursel–].

h. They must look out for _____ [themsel–].

25

a. leaves
b. beliefs
c. loaves
d. wives
e. gulfs
f. yourselves
g. ourselves
h. themselves

26   **sisters-in-law**   **major generals**

Let's see how compound nouns form their plurals.

     sister-in-law, sisters-in-law
     vice-president, vice-presidents
     commander in chief, commanders in chief
     major general, major generals

a. Which word seems more important—*vice* or *president?* _____

b. Which word seems more important—*major* or *general?* _____

c. **RULE: Compound nouns usually form their plural by adding *s* to the _____ [least/most] important word.**

26

a. *president*
b. *general*
c. most

27

Write the correct plural of the compound noun. HINT: Add *s* to the most important word.

a. He has five _____ [son-in-law].

b. Lucy waved to the _____ [passer-by].

c. Gussie had two _____ [maid of honor].

d. I faced six _____ [cross-examiner].

27

a. sons-in-law
b. passers-by
c. maids of honor
d. cross-examiners

---

28   analyses   bases

Let's see how nouns ending in *is* form their plurals.

    one analysis, two analyses
    one axis, two axes
    one basis, two bases

RULE: A singular noun ending in *is* becomes plural when the *is* is changed to _____ .

28

es

---

29   crises

Write the plurals. HINT: Change the final *is* to *es*.

crisis, _____*crises*_____   hypothesis, _____

ellipsis, _____   oasis, _____

diagnosis, _____   psychosis, _____

29

ellipses
diagnoses
hypotheses
oases
psychoses

30

Write the plurals.

a. Tom wrote two drama _____ [synopsis].

b. Dr. Schlitz approved a few _____ [thesis].

c. My aunt has several _____ [neurosis].

d. His legs look like _____ [parenthesis].

30

a. synopses
b. theses
c. neuroses
d. parentheses

31

Enter any word that you misspelled in this chapter into your Personal List of Demons in the Appendix.

REVIEW TEST: CHAPTER 8

Fill in the blanks with words studied in this chapter.

1. Most nouns—such as *dog, angel, bargain*—become plural when you add _____.

2. Nouns like *dish, match,* and *sex* that end with a hissing sound become plural when you add _____.

3. Nouns like *boy, journey,* and *delay* that end in *y* with a vowel in front of it become plural when you add _____.

4. Nouns like *army, sky,* and *enemy* that end in *y* with a consonant in front of it become plural when you change the *y* to _____ and add _____.

5. Proper nouns like *Sally* and *Haggerty* become plural when you add _____.

6. Musical terms that end in *o*—like *piano, alto,* and *cello*—become plural when you add _____.

7. Nouns like *radio, cuckoo,* and *studio* that end in *o* with a vowel in front of it become plural when you add _____.

8. Most nouns, in fact, that end in *o* become plural when you add _____.

9. About ten nouns that end in *o*—*buffalo, echo, embargo, hero, Negro, no, potato, tomato, torpedo,* and *veto*—are exceptions to the rule and become plural only when you add _____.

10. Many nouns that end in *f*—like *chef, grief,* and *serf*—become plural when you add _____.

11. Some nouns that end in *f* or *fe*—like *calf, life,* and *self*—become plurals that end in the three letters _____.

12. Compound nouns like *brother-in-law* usually become plural when you add *s* to the most _____ word.

13. Nouns like *crisis* that end in *is* become plural when you change the *is* to _____.

Write the plurals.

14. one summary, two _____

15. one week, two _____

16. one studio, two _____

17. one son-in-law, two _____

18. one monkey, two _____

19. one ditch, two _____

20. one banjo, two _____

21. one synopsis, two _____

22. one thief, two _____

23. one tomato, two _____

24. one gulf, two _____

25. one Kelly, two _____

KEY TO REVIEW TEST

Check your test answers with the following key. Deduct 4% per error from a possible 100%.

1. *s*	**6.** *s*	**11.** *ves*	**16.** studios	**21.** synopses
2. *es*	**7.** *s*	**12.** important	**17.** sons-in-law	**22.** thieves
3. *s*	**8.** *s*	**13.** *es*	**18.** monkeys	**23.** tomatoes
4. *i, es*	**9.** *es*	**14.** summaries	**19.** ditches	**24.** gulfs
5. *s*	**10.** *s*	**15.** weeks	**20.** banjos	**25.** Kellys

Score: _____ %

9

Final Silent *e*

IN THIS CHAPTER

1. accurately
2. accusing
3. achievement
4. acknowledgment
5. acreage
6. adequately
7. adoration
8. advertisement
9. advisable
10. advisory
11. argument
12. awful
13. canoeing
14. careful
15. careless
16. caring
17. changeable
18. coming
19. completely
20. conceivable
21. confusion
22. courageous
23. creation
24. definitely
25. desirous
26. donation
27. driving
28. dyeing
29. excitable
30. excitement
31. extremely
32. famous
33. having
34. hopeless
35. hoping
36. judgment
37. likely
38. liveliness
39. lively
40. living
41. lonely
42. losing
43. lovely
44. loving
45. nineteen
46. ninety
47. ninth
48. noticeable
49. opposite
50. outrageous
51. peaceable
52. provable
53. rarely
54. receivable
55. removing
56. ridiculous
57. safety
58. saving
59. seizure
60. separation
61. shapely
62. shaping
63. shining
64. shoeing
65. sincerely
66. singeing
67. singing
68. smoking
69. statement
70. surely
71. suspenseful
72. toeing
73. truly
74. useful
75. useless
76. using
77. vengeance
78. wholly
79. wisdom
80. writing

COVER THIS COLUMN

1   using   provable   famous

Note carefully what happens to the letter *e* in these combinations:

use   + ing   = using   _____   _____

prove   + able = provable   _____   _____

fame   + ous   = famous   _____   _____

donate + ion   = donation   _____   _____

a.   Words like *use, prove, fame,* and *donate* end with the silent letter

     _____ .

b.   Suffixes (endings) like *ing, able, ous,* and *ion* begin with a _____ [vowel/consonant].

c.   In a combination like *use + ing,* the *e* is _____ [kept/dropped].

d.   Go back and copy each combination word (*using,* etc.) two times.

1

a. *e*
b. vowel
c. dropped
d. [copy]

2

RULE: **When a word like *use* that ends in a silent *e* is combined with a suffix like *ing* that begins with a vowel, the *e* is_____ [kept/dropped].**

2

dropped

3

Write the answer two times.

write + ing = _____   _____

have   + ing = _____   _____

come   + ing = _____   _____

3

writing
having
coming

4

Write the words in full.

a.   The police are _____ [com–g] for Wilbur.

b.   Wilbur has been _____ [writ–g] bad checks.

c.   Those good times that Wilbur has been _____ [hav–g] are now

     _____ [com–g] to an end.

d.   Wilbur will be _____ [us–g] prison clothes.

4

a. coming
b. writing
c. having, coming
d. using

5

Write the answer two times.

conceive + able = _____ _____

separate + ion = _____ _____

adore + ation = _____ _____

desire + ous = _____ _____

5

conceivable
separation
adoration
desirous

6

Write the answer two times.

accuse + ing = _____ _____

advise + ory = _____ _____

confuse + ion = _____ _____

oppose + ite = _____ _____

6

accusing
advisory
confusion
opposite

7

REVIEW OF RULE: **When a word like** *come, adore,* **or** *desire* **that ends in a silent** _____ **is combined with a suffix like** *ing,* *ation,* **or** *ous* **that begins with a** _____, **the** *e* **is** _____.

7

e
vowel
dropped

8

Keep applying the rule about final silent *e*.

a. The sculptor is _____ [los–g] his marbles.

b. Humankind may be God's weakest _____ [creat–n].

c. Most television commercials are _____ [ridic–s].

d. A heart _____ [seiz–ure] is no picnic.

8

a. losing
b. creation
c. ridiculous
d. seizure

9   **courageous   noticeable**

EXCEPTIONS: **Note exceptions involving** *ge* **and** *ce.*

courage + ous = courageous
notice + able = noticeable

a. *Courage* and *notice* end in silent *e,* and the suffix begins with a vowel, yet the *e* is _____ [kept/dropped].

b. The *e* is kept in *courageous* so that the *g* will sound like _____ [*j*/the *g* in *gas*].

c. The *e* is kept in *noticeable* so that the *c* will sound like _____ [*s/k*].

9

a. kept
b. *j*
c. *s*

10

Write each word two times.

changeable _____ _____

courageous _____ _____

noticeable _____ _____

outrageous _____ _____

peaceable _____ _____

vengeance _____ _____

10

[copy]

11

Write the words in full.

He flung me an _____ [outrag–s] insult.

Luckily I am a _____ [peac–able] man.

If I were more _____ [courag–s], I might have vowed

_____ [veng–ce].

11

outrageous
peaceable
courageous
vengeance

12   canoeing   acreage

MORE EXCEPTIONS: A few combinations hang on to the *e* for the sake of clarity: *canoeing, dyeing, shoeing, singeing, toeing, acreage*. Copy the six exceptions.

_____ _____

_____ _____

_____ _____

12

[copy]

13

Write the words in full. Remember: These are exceptions, and they have unusual spellings for the sake of clarity.

While his bride was _____ [dy–ng] her wedding dress and

_____ [sing–ng] her hair, Clarence was _____ [cano–ng] over Niagara Falls.

13

dyeing
singeing
canoeing

14   QUIZ

Write the words in full.

a. Ike is _____ [hav–g] _____ [outrag–s] fun.

b. A _____ [courag–s] dog is _____ [sav–g] us.

c. I'm _____ [writ–g]: "Cash _____ [rec–v–ble]."

d. His mind is clean—it's _____ [chang–ble].

e. Ida was _____ [sing–g] her hair and _____ [sing–g] "Smoke Gets in Your Eyes."

14

a. having, outrageous

b. courageous, saving

c. writing, receivable

d. changeable

e. singeing, singing

15　　　useless　　　lively　　　excitement

Let's see what happens when a word like *use* that ends in a silent *e* is combined with a suffix like *less* that begins with a consonant.

use + less = useless
live + ly = lively
excite + ment = excitement

a. *Use, live,* and *excite* end in the silent letter _____.

b. The suffixes *less, ly,* and *ment* begin with a _____ [vowel/consonant].

c. In a combination like *use + less,* the silent *e* is _____ [kept/dropped].

15

a. *e*

b. consonant

c. kept

16

RULE: We keep the final silent *e* when we add a suffix that begins with a _____ [vowel/consonant].

16

consonant

17

Copy each word two times.

useless　_____　_____

lively　_____　_____

excitement _____　_____

17

[copy]

18

Write the words in full.

Honkville was not a _____ [liv–y] town, and any efforts to wake it up were _____ [us–l–s]. Our main _____ [ex–t–ment] was watching the grass grow.

18

lively
useless
excitement

19

Write the answer two times.

definite + ly =　_____　_____

lone　　+ ly =　_____　_____

sincere + ly =　_____　_____

19	20
definitely	Write the words in full.
lonely	"Bella," he wrote, "I'm so _____ [lon–y]. I _____ [def–n–ly]
sincerely	love you. _____ [Sinc–ly], Sheldon."

20	21
lonely	Write the answer two times.
definitely	advertise + ment = _____ _____
Sincerely	care + less = _____ _____
	extreme + ly = _____ _____
	like + ly = _____ _____

21	22
advertisement	Write the words in full.
careless	How _____ [car–les–]! I swallowed a frog, and I'm _____
extremely	[lik–y] to croak.
likely	

22	23
careless	Write the words in full.
likely	One _____ [car–les–] prizefighter is knocked flat so often it's
	_____ [ext–m–ly] _____ [lik–y] he can sell _____
	[adv–tis–m–nt] space on the soles of his shoes.

23	24 **argument** **judgment** **ninth**
careless	**EXCEPTIONS:** Write each word two times.
extremely	acknowledgment* _____ _____
likely	argument _____ _____
advertisement	awful _____ _____
	judgment* _____ _____
	ninth _____ _____
	truly _____ _____
	wholly _____ _____
	wisdom _____ _____
	*The British spelling has an *e* after the *g*.

24

[copy]

---

25   **QUIZ**

Write the words in full, but look out—these are the exceptions.

"Dear Bella: I am _____ [tr–ly] sorry we had that _____

[a–ful] _____ [arg–ment] on the _____ [ni–th] floor. I

shouldn't have kissed you. Accept my _____ [ackn–l–g–nt] it was

_____ [wh–ly] an error in _____ [jud–ment]. I was under

the influence of love, not _____ [wi–dom]. Yours _____

[tr–ly], Sheldon."

25

truly, awful
argument, ninth
acknowledgment
wholly
judgment
wisdom
truly

26

Write the words in full.

a. Is a priest _____ [wh–ly] holy?

b. Ed is, without _____ [arg–ment], the nicest boy in the

    _____ [ni–th] grade of the reform school.

c. This donkey has _____ [wi–dom], but nobody _____

    [tr–ly] likes a smart ass.

26

a. wholly
b. argument,
   ninth
c. wisdom,
   truly

---

27   *loving*   *lovely*

The word *love* ends in a silent *e*.

a. In *loving* we have dropped the silent *e* because the suffix *ing* begins

    with a _____ .

b. In *lovely* we hang on to the silent *e* because *ly* begins with a _____ .

c. A plain life is better than a _____ [lov–y] funeral.

27

a. vowel
b. consonant
c. lovely

28

Decide whether to drop the *e* or to hang on to it. Then write the answers
two times.

use   + ful   = _____   _____

care   + ing   = _____   _____

sure   + ly   = _____   _____

achieve + ment = _____   _____

shape   + ing   = _____   _____

28	29
useful caring surely achievement shaping	Continue as in frame 28. complete + ly = _____ _____ excite + able = _____ _____ remove + ing = _____ _____ smoke + ing = _____ _____ suspense + ful = _____ _____

29	30 QUIZ
completely excitable removing smoking suspenseful	Write the words in full. Surgeons have been _____ [remov–g] Smoky Joe's lung. Now he is _____ [compl–ly] recovered and _____ [smok–g] again with frantic _____ [liv–iness]. Smoky Joe _____ [sur–ly] is _____ [shap–ng] up.

30	31
removing completely smoking liveliness surely shaping	Continue as in frame 28. adequate + ly = _____ _____ hope + ing = _____ _____ hope + less = _____ _____ nine + teen = _____ _____ shine + ing = _____ _____

31	32
adequately hoping hopeless nineteen shining	Continue as in frame 28. accurate + ly = _____ _____ advise + able = _____ _____ live + ing = _____ _____ shape + ly = _____ _____ state + ment = _____ _____

32	33
accurately	Continue as in frame 28.
advisable	
living	care + ful = _____ _____
shapely	drive + ing = _____ _____
statement	nine + ty = _____ _____
	rare + ly = _____ _____
	safe + ty = _____ _____

33	34
careful	Write the words in full.
driving	Sad was Dad's _____ [stat–nt]: "If the rich could hire the poor to
ninety	die for them, the poor could _____ [tr–ly] make a nice _____
rarely	[liv–g]."
safety	

34	35 QUIZ
statement	Write the words in full.
truly	Grandpa is _____ [nin–y] years old, so I was shocked at his
living	_____ [stat–ent]. "I'm _____ [mar–ing] a _____
	[shap–ly] girl of _____ [ni–teen]," he said, "and if she stays
	_____ [compl–t–y] healthy, we'll buy a house near the elementary
	school and be _____ [liv–g] happily ever after."

35	36
ninety	Enter any words that you misspelled in this chapter into your Personal
statement	List of Demons in the Appendix.
marrying	
shapely	
nineteen	
completely	
living	

Fill in the blanks with words studied in this chapter.

1. Linus hit a tree on his way to _____ [driv–g] school.

2. The stranger promised _____ [sinc–ly] to cure the cancer.

3. Custer was _____ [hop–ul] that he could defeat the Indians.

4. That's a pretty good andante _____ [mov–nt], Mr. Mozart.

5. Nobody is _____ [compl–t–y] without sin, not even I.

6. Carla is _____ [dy–ng] her shoes to match her lipstick.

7. The psychiatrist and his wife had a violent _____ [arg–nt].

8. When Papa drives, I quickly fasten my _____ [saf–y] belt.

9. The skunk wonders why he is _____ [lon–y].

10. Santa Claus is _____ [com–ng] on a bicycle.

11. Welcome to _____ [lov–ly] Smogtown.

12. Greg is studying the _____ [mat–ng] habits of the octopus.

13. The _____ [courag–s] matador climbed off the fence.

14. Add good grammar, for variety, to your _____ [writ–ng].

15. Is my black eye _____ [notic–ble]?

16. Stop _____ [us–ng] my toothbrush to clean the typewriter keys.

17. She has splendid _____ [jud–ment]—she admires me.

18. Hamlet was hit by arrows of _____ [outrag–s] fortune.

19. And what's your _____ [griev–ce]?

20. Nick and his father fight like labor and _____ [manag–nt].

21. The seed catalogues filled Pam with _____ [excit–ent].

22. The clown was _____ [div–ng] into a pail of water.

23. That bulldog doesn't look _____ [peac–ble].

24. Every war, he says, is a _____ [los–ng] war.

25. Pat got a job _____ [shap–ng] pretzels.

KEY TO REVIEW TEST

Check your test answers with the following key. Deduct 4% per error from a possible 100%.

1. driving	**6.** dyeing	**11.** lovely	**16.** using	**21.** excitement
2. sincerely	**7.** argument	**12.** mating	**17.** judgment	**22.** diving
3. hopeful	**8.** safety	**13.** courageous	**18.** outrageous	**23.** peaceable
4. movement	**9.** lonely	**14.** writing	**19.** grievance	**24.** losing
5. completely	**10.** coming	**15.** noticeable	**20.** management	**25.** shaping

Score: _____%

10

Fight Those Demons! (36–70)

IN THIS CHAPTER

36. courage	43. daughter	50. dictionary	57. doesn't	64. environment
37. cousin	44. deceive	51. difference	58. dollar	65. escape
38. coward	45. decision	52. disappear	59. dozen	66. everybody
39. creature	46. definite	53. discussion	60. drowned	67. exercise
40. cruelty	47. delicious	54. divide	61. during	68. February
41. curious	48. description	55. divine	62. easily	69. friendly
42. customer	49. desperate	56. doctor	63. education	70. grammar

COVER THIS COLUMN

1	courage	cousin	coward	creature
	cruelty	curious	customer	

Copy each demon two times, first in print, then in handwriting. Memorize as you write.

	Print	Handwriting
courage		
cousin		
coward		
creature		
cruelty		
curious		
customer		

1	2
[copy]	Write the words in full. Only a _____ [c–w–r–d–] inflicts _____ [c–r–u–l–t–] on a helpless _____ [c–r–e–t–r–]. In a _____ [c–r–i–u–s–] act of _____ [c–r–a–g–e], my _____ [c–u–s–n–] prevented a pet store _____ [c–s–t–m–r–] from torturing a collie.

2	3
coward cruelty creature curious courage cousin customer	Write the words in full. My _____ [c–u–s–n–] is no _____ [c–w–r–d], but he's not noted for his _____ [c–r–a–g–e] either. When he saw a _____ [c–u–r–u–s–] _____ [c–r–e–t–r–] in a swamp, he said, "What an ugly _____ [c–u–s–t–m–r–]! Such _____ [c–r–u–l–t–] in those jaws!"

3	4
cousin coward courage curious creature customer cruelty	PROOFREADING. Cross out any misspelled words and write the correct spelling above them. How curious it is that a wimpy creture like my cousin, whom I regarded as a cowerd, can rise to acts of courage. Spotting crulety, he becomes a tough customer, an avenger.

4	5
creature coward cruelty	**daughter** **deceive** **decision** **definite** **delicious** **description** **desperate** Copy each demon two times, first in print, then in handwriting. Memorize as you write. <table><tr><td></td><td>Print</td><td>Handwriting</td></tr><tr><td>daughter</td><td>_____</td><td>_____</td></tr><tr><td>deceive</td><td>_____</td><td>_____</td></tr><tr><td>decision</td><td>_____</td><td>_____</td></tr><tr><td>definite</td><td>_____</td><td>_____</td></tr><tr><td>delicious</td><td>_____</td><td>_____</td></tr><tr><td>description</td><td>_____</td><td>_____</td></tr><tr><td>desperate</td><td>_____</td><td>_____</td></tr></table>

5

[copy]

6

Write the words in full.

The chef made a _____ [d–e–f–n–t–e] _____ [d–e–c–s–n–] to _____ [d–e–c–v–e] my _____ [d–a–t–r]. He was _____ [d–e–s–p–r–t–] to get a _____ [d–s–c–r–t–n] of the recipe for her _____ [d–e–l–i–s–] soup.

6

definite
decision
deceive
daughter
desperate
description
delicious

7

Write the words in full.

My _____ [d–a–t–r] gave me a _____ [d–e–f–n–t–e] _____ [d–s–c–r–t–n] of how she made her _____ [d–e–l–i–s–] soup. Her _____ [d–e–c–s–n–] was to _____ [d–e–c–v–e] the sneaky, _____ [d–e–s–p–r–t] chef and give him a faulty recipe.

7

daughter
definite
description
delicious
decision
deceive
desperate

8

PROOFREADING. Cross out any misspelled words and write the correct spelling above them.

My daughter, you make delicous soup. That's definate. Your soup is beyond description. Why would I deceive you? I'm desparate to have another bowl. It's a decision I won't regret.

8

delicious
definite
desperate

9

| dictionary | difference | disappear | discussion |
| divide | divine | doctor | |

Copy each demon two times, first in print, then in handwriting. Memorize as you write.

	Print	Handwriting
dictionary	_____	_____
difference	_____	_____
disappear	_____	_____
discussion	_____	_____
divide	_____	_____
divine	_____	_____
doctor	_____	_____

9

[copy]

10

Write the words in full.

My _____ [d–s–c–u–s–n] with the _____ [d–o–c–t–r]

resulted in a _____ [d–i–f–r–n–c–] as to the meaning of

_____ [d–v–i–n–] healing. Where did my _____

[d–i–c–t–r–y] _____ [d–i–s–p–e–r–]? Small disputes shouldn't

_____ [d–v–i–d–e] friends.

10

discussion
doctor
difference
divine
dictionary
disappear
divide

11

Write the words in full.

Many a _____ [d–i–f–r–n–c–] of opinion in a _____

[d–s–c–u–s–n–] can _____ [d–v–i–d–] people; but consulting a

_____ [d–i–c–n–r–y] can make disputes _____ [d–i–s–p–r–].

Webster's is almost a _____ [d–v–i–n–] solution—just what the

_____ [d–c–t–r–] ordered.

11

difference
discussion
divide
dictionary
disappear
divine
doctor

12

PROOFREADING. Cross out any misspelled words and write the correct
spelling above them.

Lucy felt that skin cream would make a diference in her looks. But Lucy's

doctor said her wrinkles won't disappear without devine help. Discussion

served only to divide the two. Lucy finally banged the docter's head with a

heavy dictionary.

12

difference
divine
doctor's

13 | doesn't | dollar | dozen | drowned
during | easily | education

Copy each demon two times, first in print, then in handwriting. Memorize
as you write.

	Print	Handwriting
doesn't	_____	_____
dollar	_____	_____
dozen	_____	_____
drowned	_____	_____
during	_____	_____

easily _____ _____

education _____ _____

13

[copy]

14

Write the words in full.

Things were cheap _____ [d–r–i–n–g–] the '30s and one could

_____ [e–s–l–y–] afford a college _____ [e–d–c–a–t–n].

Today a _____ [d–o–l–r–] _____ [d–o–s–n–t] buy a

_____ [d–z–n–] jellybeans and most citizens are _____
[d–r–w–n–d] in debt.

14

during
easily
education
dollar
doesn't
dozen
drowned

15

Write the words in full.

Sam _____ [d–o–s–n–t] earn a _____ [d–o–l–r] toward his

_____ [e–d–c–a–t–n] _____ [d–u–r–n–g] the summer. His

sister Sue, however, _____ [e–s–l–y] gets work as a lifeguard and

rescues a _____ [d–z–n] fellows who might have _____
[d–r–w–n–d].

15

doesn't
dollar
education
during
easily
dozen
drowned

16

PROOFREADING. Cross out any misspelled words and write the correct
spelling above them.

Percy had a duzen years of edication, but he doesn't now the value of a

dollar. He spends too easly durning a shopping spree and is then drowned

in unpaid bills.

16

dozen
education
know
easily
during

17   **environment**   **escape**   **everybody**   **exercise**
          February   **friendly**   **grammar**

Copy each demon two times, first in print, then in handwriting. Memorize
as you write.

	Print	Handwriting
environment	_____	_____
escape	_____	_____
everybody	_____	_____
exercise	_____	_____

February	_____ _____
friendly	_____ _____
grammar	_____ _____

17

[copy]

18

Write the words in full.

Scarface didn't like the prison _____ [e–n–v–r–m–n–t]. He desired something more _____ [f–r–n–d–l–y]. He managed to _____ [e–c–a–p–e] one morning in _____ [F–e–b–r–y] when _____ [e–v–r–b–d–y] else was busily taking part in prison _____ [e–x–r–i–s–e]. How was Scarface recognized and caught? He posed as a college professor, but his _____ [g–r–a–m–r] gave him away.

18

environment
friendly
escape
February
everybody
exercise
grammar

19

Write the words in full.

Rosita liked her _____ [g–r–a–m–r] class. _____ [E–v–r–b–d–y] was very _____ [f–r–n–d–l–y]. She handled each writing _____ [e–x–r–i–s–e] without trouble and looked forward to graduation in _____ [F–e–b–r–y]. With a diploma Rosita hoped to _____ [e–c–a–p–e] into a more promising labor _____ [e–n–v–r–m–n–t].

19

grammar
Everybody
friendly
exercise
February
escape
environment

20

PROOFREADING. Cross out any misspelled words and write the correct spelling above them.

The Arctic in Febuary is not the ideal envirement for physical exercise. Almost everybody would be glad to escape for a few weeks to a more friendly climate. The natives often cursed the blizzards in grammer as horrendous as the storms themselves.

20

February
environment
grammar

21

Enter any words that you misspelled in this chapter into your Personal List of Demons in the Appendix.

REVIEW TEST: CHAPTER 10

Fill in the blanks with words studied in this chapter.

1. "Sweetheart," breathed Luigi, "you are _____ [d–v–n–e]."

2. Our presidents preferred to be born in _____ [F–e–b–r–y].

3. Eggs are so cheap it _____ [d–o–s–n–t] pay to lay them.

4. The _____ [c–s–t–m–e–r] is nearly always right.

5. Most criminals have had little _____ [e–d–c–a–t–n].

6. Joe certainly made food _____ [d–i–s–p–e–r–].

7. Their war plan was to _____ [d–v–d–e] and conquer.

8. The boozer was taken home by his _____ [d–a–t–e–r].

9. Noah said the rain would be a _____ [d–e–f–i–n–t–] soaker.

10. If my heart were as bad as my _____ [g–r–a–m–r], I'd be dead.

11. Give us a _____ [d–s–c–r–t–i–n] of the killer.

12. You aren't allowed to marry your first _____ [c–u–s–n–].

13. Many who say "I'll bet a _____ [d–o–l–r]" don't have one.

14. Al brought a _____ [d–z–n] ripe tomatoes to the rally.

15. Consult your _____ [d–i–c–t–n–r–y]. Don't just sit on it.

16. As the flames approached, Nan became _____ [d–e–s–p–r–t–].

17. Our guests snored _____ [d–u–r–n–g] the night.

18. My _____ [d–o–c–t–r–] can't stand being around sick people.

19. Pat fell into the beer and _____ [d–r–o–w–d] with a grin.

20. Every _____ [c–r–e–t–r–e] has a right to live.

21. Should I be a live _____ [c–o–w–r–d] or a dead hero?

22. Ike made a _____ [d–e–c–s–n–] to become a monk.

23. Is _____ [e–v–r–b–d–y] happy?

24. We must not pollute our _____ [e–n–v–i–r–m–n–t].

25. I enjoy _____ [–x–r–c–s–e] . . . in very limited amounts.

KEY TO REVIEW TEST

Check your answers with the following key. Deduct 4% per error from a possible 100%.

1. divine	**6.** disappear	**11.** description	**16.** desperate	**21.** coward
2. February	**7.** divide	**12.** cousin	**17.** during	**22.** decision
3. doesn't	**8.** daughter	**13.** dollar	**18.** doctor	**23.** everybody
4. customer	**9.** definite	**14.** dozen	**19.** drowned	**24.** environment
5. education	**10.** grammar	**15.** dictionary	**20.** creature	**25.** exercise

Score: _____%

11

Write *i* Before *e*, Except . . .

IN THIS CHAPTER

COVER THIS COLUMN | **1**   **relief**   **receive**   **neighbor**

Let's take a close look at one of the most famous and useful of spelling jingles.

JINGLE	EXAMPLES
Write *i* before *e*	IE: believe, brief, field, grief, niece, piece, priest, relief, shriek, siege, thief
Except after *c*	CEI: ceiling, conceit, conceive, deceive, perceive, receive
Or when sounded like *a*	EI: eight, freight, heinous, reign, sleigh, veil, vein, weight
As in *neighbor* and *weigh*.	

a. The first two lines of the jingle deal with words like *thief* and *receive* that have _____ [ee/a] sounds.

b. The last two lines of the jingle deal with words like *neighbor* and *weigh* that have _____ [ee/a] sounds.

1 a. *ee* b. *a*	**2** **GENERAL RULE** (first line of the jingle): **When the sound is *ee*, we usually write _____ before _____ .**
2 *i, e*	**3** achieve Apply the general rule. If the sound is *ee*, write the *i* before the *e*. Write each word in full three times. ach–ve *achieve* _____ _____ bel–ve _____ _____ _____ ch–f _____ _____ _____ f–ld _____ _____ _____
3 believe chief field	**4** Let's repeat that general rule: We usually spell the *ee* sound with an _____ [ie/ei].
4 *ie*	**5** Write each word in full three times. gr–f _____ _____ _____ hyg–ne _____ _____ _____ n–ce _____ _____ _____ pr–st _____ _____ _____
5 grief hygiene niece priest	**6** Write words that have an *ee* sound. a. Stay away from that dope _____ [f–nd]. b. Give Jake a _____ [p–ce] of the Limburger. c. Cablegrams cost money, so be _____ [br–f].

6

a. fiend
b. piece
c. brief

7

Continue using the general rule for *ee* sounds.
Write each word in full three times.

rel–f   _____   _____   _____

shr–k   _____   _____   _____

s–ge   _____   _____   _____

th–f   _____   _____   _____

y–ld   _____   _____   _____

7

relief
shriek
siege
thief
yield

8

Continue using the general rule for *ee* sounds.
Write the words in full.

The _____ [n–ce] of the _____ [pr–st] let out a _____

[br–f] _____ [shr–k], I _____ [bel–ve], when the _____

[ch–f] _____ [th–f] came to _____ [gr–f].

8

niece
priest
brief
shriek
believe
chief
thief
grief

---

9   perceive

Line 2 of the jingle says: "Except after *c*." This means that after *c* we write *ei*. This is true, as we have seen, for *perceive, receive,* and similar words with an *ee* sound.

Write each word in full three times.

c–ling   _____   _____   _____

conc–ve   _____   _____   _____

9

ceiling
conceive

10

To repeat—line 2 of the jingle tells us that after the letter *c* we write

_____ [*ie/ei*].

10

ei

11

In other words, a common three-letter combination beginning with *c* is

_____ .

11

cei

---

12   –cei–

The letters CEI usually go together like the three musketeers.
Memorize them; say the letters aloud ten times: C   E   I.

Now, write each word in full three times.

conc–t   _____   _____   _____

dec–ve   _____   _____   _____

rec–pt   _____   _____   _____

12

conceit
deceive
receipt

13

Write words that have an *ee* sound.

a.   Dad saw my *F*'s and hit the _____ [c–ling].

b.   Sam _____ [rec–ved] ten cents every day.

c.   Our _____ [ch–f] _____ [conc–ved} an escape plan.

13

a. ceiling
b. received
c. chief,
    conceived

14   **weigh**

Lines 3 and 4 of the jingle say: "Or when sounded like *a*, as in *neighbor* and *weigh*."

This means that the *a* sound is spelled with an _____ [*ie/ei*].

14

ei

15

The words in the next frame have an *a* sound (as in *weigh*), so we will spell

them with an _____ [*ie/ei*].

15

ei

16

Write each word in full three times.

f–gn   _____   _____   _____

h–nous _____   _____   _____

r–gn   _____   _____   _____

r–n   _____   _____   _____

v–n   _____   _____   _____

v–l   _____   _____   _____

w–ght   _____   _____   _____

16

feign
heinous
reign
rein
vein
veil
weight

17

Fill in the blanks.

a.   The *a* sound as in *neighbor* and *weigh* is spelled with an _____ [*ie/ei*].

b.   I want a one-horse open _____ [sl–gh].

c.   Hobo Hank left by _____ [fr–ght] train.

17

a. *ei*
b. sleigh
c. freight

18

Continue writing the words in full.

Sam is trying to meet the pretty _____ [n–ghbor] who moved in next door. He mowed his lawn _____ [–ght] days in a row, losing some _____ [w–ght], and has the shortest grass in town.

18

neighbor
eight
weight

19

Let's review the jingle rules.

a. The *ee* sound is usually spelled with the _____ before the _____ .

b. But after *c* we write _____ [*ie/ei*].

c. For the sound of *a* we also write _____ [*ie/ei*].

19

a. *i, e.*
b. *ei*
c. *ei*

---

20   QUIZ

Write the words in full, using the jingle rules.

a. sh–ld _____   f. conc–t _____

b. rec–ve _____   g. w–ght _____

c. v–n   _____   h. y–ld _____

d. f–ld _____   i. perc–ve _____

e. th–f _____   j. n–ghbor _____

20

a. shield
b. receive
c. vein
d. field
e. thief
f. conceit
g. weight
h. yield
i. perceive
j. neighbor

---

21   leisure   seize   weird

EXCEPTIONS: The following are exceptions to the jingle rules. Examine them closely.

Write each word three times.

either   _____   _____   _____

financier _____   _____   _____

leisure _____   _____   _____

neither _____   _____   _____

seize   _____   _____   _____

sheik   _____   _____   _____

weird   _____   _____   _____

21

[copy]

22

Write the exceptions in full.

a. I don't trust _____ [–ther] candidate.

b. Mother gets no _____ [l–sure] on Mother's Day.

c. Casper has two cars, but _____ [n–ther] one can move without _____ [w–rd] noises.

22

a. either
b. leisure
c. neither,
   weird

23

Review of exceptions: Memorize the following sentence; then write it two times.

Neither of the financiers, nor the weird sheik either, can seize leisure.

1. _____

    _____

2. _____

    _____

23

[copy]

24

Continue writing the exceptions in full.

a. Sally sang "The _____ [Sh–k] of Araby," and she sounded pretty _____ [w–rd].

b. If that _____ [finan–r] sees my car, he'll _____ [s–ze] my car.

24

a. Sheik,
   weird
b. financier,
   seize

---

25   **Fahrenheit   foreign   science**

The four-line jingle that begins "Write *i* before *e*" is very helpful, as we have seen, in the spelling of *ee* sounds and *a* sounds. **But the jingle does not apply to other sounds,** as in the words that follow. These oddball spellings must simply be memorized.

Write these words two times.

ancient	_____	_____
counterfeit	_____	_____
efficient	_____	_____
Fahrenheit	_____	_____
foreign	_____	_____
forfeit	_____	_____
height	_____	_____

heir _____ _____

science _____ _____

sovereign _____ _____

sufficient _____ _____

25 [copy]	**26** ancient sufficient Examine the words *ancient, conscience, efficient, proficient,* and *sufficient.* Notice that none of them have an *ee* sound, but that they all have an *sh* sound. Evidently, when *c* is pronounced like *sh,* it is followed by the letters _____ [ie/ei].
26 *ie*	**27** The words that follow do not have an *ee* or an *a* sound, so they do not go by the jingle rules. Write the words in full. a. Huxley was a man of _____ [sc–nce]. b. That three-dollar bill might be _____ [counterf–t].
27 a. science b. counterfeit	**28** Continue as in frame 27. a. I was swindled in _____ [effic–nt] fashion. b. Tom Thumb ate string beans to gain _____ [h–ght].
28 a. efficient b. height	**29** Continue as in frame 27. a. Wow! Forty below, _____ [Fahrenh–t]! b. The millionaire gave his _____ [h–r] the air. c. My dog is learning a _____ [for–gn] language. He says, "Meow!" d. My car is so _____ [anc–nt] that Medicare pays 80% of repair bills. That's hardly _____ [suffic–nt].
29 a. Fahrenheit b. heir c. foreign d. ancient, sufficient	**30** Enter any words that you misspelled in this chapter into your Personal List of Demons in the Appendix.

Decide—*ie* or *ei*. Then write each word in full.

1. Tarzan's _____ [n–ghbor] was a gorilla named Irving.

2. These natives _____ [bel–ve] that hard work is a sin.

3. Spend your _____ [l–sure] time in the library.

4. My nurse didn't know a _____ [v–n] from an artery.

5. They hanged the cattle _____ [th–f] to reform him.

6. I bought a wolf to _____ [sh–ld] my hens from harm.

7. Joe earned a *D* in his best subject, _____ [sc–nce].

8. Will six eggs be _____ [suffic–nt] for lunch?

9. Her _____ [n–ce] was elected to Phi Beta Kappa.

10. That _____ [anc–nt] skull is from a politician—the jaws are open.

11. The little _____ [for–gn] car hit my kneecap.

12. A zebra is a horse in _____ [w–rd] pajamas.

13. If you wait, I'll guess your _____ [w–ght].

14. Boris bit the _____ [counterf–t] quarter.

15. We've bought a _____ [f–ld] of cactus!

16. Losing his cow filled Gaston with _____ [gr–f].

17. Only Hercules could _____ [w–ld] that sword.

18. This dental _____ [rec–pt] for a dollar? I have buck teeth.

19. Each admiral dreams of sinking a few _____ [nav–s].

20. His bragging wouldn't _____ [dec–ve] a boy of four.

21. The Indian _____ [ch–f] was cheated by palefaces.

22. Did you ever _____ [rec–ve] a small hospital bill?

23. Life was _____ [br–f] for the drug addict.

24. If anybody sees him, _____ [s–ze] him.

25. Phil enjoyed _____ [n–ther] his mumps nor his malaria.

KEY TO REVIEW TEST

Check your test answers with the following key. Deduct 4% per error from a possible 100%.

1. neighbor	**6.** shield	**11.** foreign	**16.** grief	**21.** chief
2. believe	**7.** science	**12.** weird	**17.** wield	**22.** receive
3. leisure	**8.** sufficient	**13.** weight	**18.** receipt	**23.** brief
4. vein	**9.** niece	**14.** counterfeit	**19.** navies	**24.** seize
5. thief	**10.** ancient	**15.** field	**20.** deceive	**25.** neither

Score: _____ %

12

Doubling the Final Consonant

IN THIS CHAPTER

COVER THIS COLUMN

1

Let's review the vowels and consonants.

a. The letters *a, e, i, o, u,* and sometimes *y* are called _____.

b. The other letters of the alphabet—such as *b, k, m, p, t, w*—are called

_____ .

129

1 a. vowels b. consonants	**2** Circle the vowels. e b j o u p l k a f r z i m
2 Circle: *e, o, u, a, i*	**3** Circle the consonants. g i c n o e t v a i s e o u
3 Circle: *g, c, n, t, v, s*	**4** Circle the words that end in a single consonant that follows a single vowel (examples: *grab, drip, permit*). dream bloom cramp throb spaghetti begin conflict slug strength
4 Circle: *throb* *slug* *begin*	**5** Circle the suffixes (word endings) that begin with a vowel. ing ly lorn ful ment ness er able less ed
5 Circle: *ing* *er* *able* *ed*	**6** **bigger** **dropped** **planning** Some one-syllable words double their final consonant when a suffix like *ed* or *ing* is added. bi*g* + er = bi*gg*er (The *g* is doubled.) dro*p* + ed = dro*pp*ed (The *p* is doubled.) pla*n* + ing = pla*nn*ing (The *n* is doubled.) a. Examine the words *big, drop,* and *plan.* They all end in a single _____ [vowel/consonant]. b. Again examine *big, drop,* and *plan.* In front of that single final consonant there is a single _____. c. The suffixes *er, ed,* and *ing,* which were added, all begin with a _____ [vowel/consonant].
6 a. consonant b. vowel c. vowel	**7** bi*g* + er = bi*gg*er In other words, the one-syllable word *big* ends in a single consonant that follows a single vowel. But before we add *er* to *big,* we must _____ [double/not double] the *g*.

7 double	**8** dro*p* + ed = dro*pp*ed The one-syllable word *drop* also ends in a single consonant that follows a single _____ . But before we add *ed* to *drop,* we must _____ the *p.*
8 vowel double	**9** pla*n* + ing = pla*nn*ing The one-syllable word *plan* also ends in a single _____ that follows a single _____ . So before we add *ing* to *plan,* we must _____ the *n.*
9 consonant vowel double	**10** RULE: **A one syllable word—like *big, drop,* or *plan*—that ends in a** **single _____ that follows a single _____ must double** **its final consonant before adding a suffix such as *er, ed,* or *ing*** **that begins with a _____ [vowel/consonant].**
10 consonant vowel vowel	**11** **ripping** Add the suffix, according to the rule, and write the new word three times. rip + ing = *ripping* _____ _____ flat + est = _____ _____ grip + ed = _____ _____ slim + er = _____ _____ snap + y = _____ _____
11 flattest gripped slimmer snappy	**12** Continue as in frame 11. blab + ing = _____ _____ flap + able = _____ _____

rob   + er   = _____

_____

step   + ed   = _____

_____

swim + ing = _____

_____

12

blabbing
flappable
robber
stepped
swimming

13

Continue as in frame 11.

dig   + ing = _____

_____

flip + ed   = _____

_____

sad + er   = _____

_____

sum + ary = _____

_____

writ + en   = _____

_____

13

digging
flipped
sadder
summary
written

14

Write the past tense of the bracketed word.

a. The butcher _____ [wrap] the bologna.

b. Mrs. Moody _____ [stir] the crab soup.

c. This red-headed boy _____ [flag] the train. He really

     _____ [use] his head.

d. My cereal _____ [snap], crackled, and _____ [pop].

14

a. wrapped
b. stirred
c. flagged,
   used
d. snapped,
   popped

15   **omitting**   **rebelling**   **furthering**

Doubling also takes place in longer words if their accent is on the last syllable, just before the suffix.

        o-MIT + ing   = o-MIT-ting   (*t* is doubled)
        re-BEL + ing   = re-BEL-ling   (*l* is doubled)
        FUR-ther + ing = FUR-ther-ing   (*r* is not doubled)

The doubling occurs only in the words that _____ [are/aren't] accented just before the suffix.

15 are	**16**　**THE VAC TEST** Suppose we want to write the past tense of a word like *commit*. We have to decide whether or not to double the *t* before adding *ed*—so let's use the VAC test, which is as follows. A V△C <u>c　o　m　-　m　i　t</u> + <u>e　d</u> = ? Imagine a little triangle VAC just above the end of the word *commit*. 　　　　V stands for single Vowel 　　　　A stands for Accent 　　　　C stands for final single Consonant Does the syllable *mit* have all three things that VAC stands for? _____ If so, we double the final consonant. Fill the blank: 　　　commit + ed = _____
16 yes committed	**17** Suppose we want to write the past tense of *refer*. Let's use the VAC test. A V△C <u>r　e　-　f　e　r</u> + <u>e　d</u> = ? Imagine a little triangle VAC just above the end of the word *refer*. Does the syllable *fer* have all three things that VAC stands for—the single Vowel, the Accent, and the final single Consonant? _____ If so, we double the final consonant. Fill the blank: 　　　refer + ed = _____
17 yes referred	**18** **VAC stands for <u>V</u>_____ , <u>A</u>_____ , <u>C</u>_____ . When all three are present, the final consonant is doubled before suffixes like *ed* and *ing* that begin with a _____ .**
18 Vowel Accent Consonant vowel	**19** Use the VAC test on the following words to make sure the final consonant has to be doubled. Write each answer two times. admit　+ ed　= _____　_____ confer　+ ing　= _____　_____ compel + ed　= _____　_____

19 admitted conferring compelled	**20** Continue as in frame 19. occur + ence = _____ _____ submit + ing = _____ _____ repel + ent = _____ _____
20 occurrence submitting repellent	**21** Apply the VAC test; then write the past tense of the bracketed words. a. The test tubes _____ [emit] a foul smell. b. My counselor _____ [confer] with me for ten minutes, then _____ [commit] suicide. c. Could I have my induction _____ [defer]?
21 a. emitted b. conferred, committed c. deferred	**22** Apply the VAC test to the words *flash, green, sink,* and *surround.* a. Do these words end in a single consonant that follows a single vowel? _____ b. If not, should their final consonant be doubled before a suffix? _____ c. Fill in the blanks. flash + ed = _flashed_____ green + er = _____ sink + ing = _____ surround + ing = _____

22
 	
a. no
b. no
c. greener
     sinking
     surrounding
	23
	
	Apply the VAC test to the words *fasten, model, murder,* and *benefit.*
	
	a. Do these words have their accent on the last syllable? _____
	
	b. If not, should their final consonant be doubled? _____
	
	c. Fill in the blanks.
	
	fasten + ed = _fastened_____
	
	model + ed = _____
	
	murder + ed = _____
	
	benefit + ed = _____

23	24	**preferred**	**preference**

23

a. no
b. no
c. modeled
   murdered
   benefited

---

24   **preferred**   **preference**

Apply the VAC test to the words that follow. Notice how a shift in accent can affect the doubling of a consonant.

Write the second word of the pair two times.

confer, conferred   _____   _____

confer, conference   _____   _____

prefer, preferred   _____   _____

prefer, preference   _____   _____

refer, referred   _____   _____

refer, reference   _____   _____

24

[copy]

---

25   **transferred**   **transferring**

The noun *transfer* is accented on the first syllable (Give me a TRANS-fer); but the verb *transfer* is accented on the second syllable (Please trans-FER this trash).

Apply the VAC test and fill in the blanks.

a. Amy _____ [transfer + ed] to a bus.

b. We had a job _____ [transfer + ing] Trudy's bull fiddle in the VW.

c. Mr. Shlepp _____ [transfer + ed] a sack of manure, and now he is _____ [transfer + ing] another sack.

25

a. transferred
b. transferring
c. transferred,
   transferring

---

26   **QUIZ**

Write the past tenses.

a. omit, *omitted*   f. flush, _____

b. refer, _____   g. transfer, _____

c. benefit, _____   h. drop, _____

d. climb, _____   i. limp, _____

e. grip, _____   j. occur, _____

26	27 acquittal equipping quizzed
b. referred c. benefited d. climbed e. gripped f. flushed g. transferred h. dropped i. limped j. occurred	The letter *u* in *occur* is a vowel, but the letter *u* in *quit* has the sound of *w* and is considered to be a consonant. Let's apply the VAC test accordingly. $$\text{quit} + \text{ing} = \text{quitting}$$ Write each answer in full two times. acquit + al = _____ _____ equip + ing = _____ _____ quiz + ed = _____ _____
27 acquittal equipping quizzed	**28** committed commitment To double the *t* or not to double the *t*—that is the question. $$\text{commit} + \text{ed} = \text{committed}$$ $$\text{commit} + \text{ment} = \text{commitment}$$ The *t* is doubled in *committed*. However, the *t* _____ [is/is not] doubled in *commitment* because the suffix *ment* begins with a _____ [vowel/consonant]. Hamlet's uncle _____ [com–t–d] an evil deed.
28 is not consonant committed	**29** Apply the VAC test for doubling and keep your eye on the suffix, too. Write each answer two times. allot + ed = _____ _____ allot + ment = _____ _____ hot + ly = _____ _____ hot + er = _____ _____ commit + ing = _____ _____
29 allotted allotment hotly hotter committing	**30** Write the past tenses. a. I was _____ [rob]! b. The lifeguard _____ [grasp] me by the hair. c. The red-nosed reindeer _____ [admit] he drank a little. d. We had a _____ [heat] argument in the boiler room. e. The robbery _____ [occur] during the police parade.

30

a. robbed
b. grasped
c. admitted
d. heated
e. occurred

31

Fill in the blanks with words ending in *ing*.

a. Papa was _____ [emit] a loud snore.

b. The sign "Fine for _____ [spit]" is not an invitation.

c. Stop _____ [splash] ink on my white suit.

d. Was _____ [split] the atom a wise crack?

e. My boss is _____ [dream] of a green Christmas.

f. You aren't _____ [make] footprints in the sands of time by _____ [sit] down.

31

a. emitting
b. spitting
c. splashing
d. splitting
e. dreaming
f. making,
   sitting

32

Enter any words that you misspelled in this chapter into your Personal List of Demons in the Appendix.

Fill in the blanks with words studied in this chapter.

1. Some crazy raven is _____ [tap–ng] at my chamber door.

2. The sergeant _____ [transfer–d] me to kitchen duty.

3. In the bookshelf of life, God is a useful _____ [refer–nce].

4. My new car is _____ [begin–g] to drop oil.

5. Time _____ [blur–d] his memory of his lover's name.

6. King Lear had trouble _____ [control–g] his temper.

7. Ship us an _____ [allot–nt] of blonde wigs.

8. Smart writers keep _____ [refer–g] to dictionaries.

9. Eva is a model of physical _____ [fit–ness].

10. What happens to a dream _____ [defer–d]?

11. Slim _____ [commit–d] five murders and a parking violation.

12. The actress was well _____ [equip–d] for her role.

13. Has our local smog _____ [ben–f–t–d] your lungs?

14. At night the air gets _____ [nip–y].

15. Write a detailed _____ [sum–ry] of *War and Peace.*

16. Nick is _____ [swim–g] in the polluted pool.

17. The draftee asked for a _____ [defer–nt].

18. I wouldn't advise _____ [drop–g] that dynamite.

19. Snavely claims he was at the _____ [confer–ce].

20. My candidate makes _____ [big–r] promises.

21. The men were _____ [snicker–g] at a crude joke.

22. The principal _____ [grab–d] me by the ears.

23. Are the British people _____ [snob–sh]?

24. Snake soup or snails? What's your _____ [prefer–ce]?

25. Wonderful! You haven't _____ [omit–d] a comma.

KEY TO REVIEW TEST

Check your test answers with the following key. Deduct 4% per error from a possible 100%.

1. tapping	**6.** controlling	**11.** committed	**16.** swimming	**21.** snickering
2. transferred	**7.** allotment	**12.** equipped	**17.** deferment	**22.** grabbed
3. reference	**8.** referring	**13.** benefited	**18.** dropping	**23.** snobbish
4. beginning	**9.** fitness	**14.** nippy	**19.** conference	**24.** preference
5. blurred	**10.** deferred	**15.** summary	**20.** bigger	**25.** omitted

Score: _____%

13

Fight Those Demons!
(71–105)

IN THIS CHAPTER

COVER THIS COLUMN

1

group	guarantee	happiness	headache
health	heaven	hundred	

Copy each demon two times, first in print, then in handwriting. Memorize as you write.

	Print	Handwriting
group	_____	_____
guarantee	_____	_____
happiness	_____	_____
headache	_____	_____
health	_____	_____
heaven	_____	_____
hundred	_____	_____

1 [copy]	**2** Write the words in full. We _____ [g–a–r–n–t–e–] _____ [h–e–l–t–] and _____ [h–a–p–n–e–s–] to users of Zingo, our new _____ [h–e–d–a–c–] pill. Zingo is first choice of a _____ [g–r–u–p–] of doctors. Get one _____ [h–u–d–r–d] Zingos in a bottle, and _____ [h–e–v–n] can wait.
2 guarantee health happiness headache group hundred heaven	**3** Write the words in full. I get a _____ [h–e–d–a–c–] just watching TV _____ [h–e–l–t–] ads. How can a trampoline _____ [g–a–r–n–t–e–] my _____ [h–a–p–n–e–s–]? I've sat through a _____ [h–u–n–d–r–d] commercials dealing with exercise machines and— _____ [h–e–v–n–] forbid!—here comes another _____ [g–r–u–p–].
3 headache health guarantee happiness hundred heaven group	**4** PROOFREADING. Cross out any misspelled words and write the correct spelling above them. We are a group of one hunderd plumbers. Getting health insurance for us hasn't been a pipe job; in fact, it's been a clogging headake. That's why your guarantee of coverage sounds like heaven and has brought us a flood of happyness.

4
 	
hundred
headache
happiness
	5 **hungry incredible independent instead**
	              interesting interrupt introduce
	
	Copy each demon two times, first in print, then in handwriting. Memorize as you write.
	
	                   Print Handwriting
	
	hungry _____ _____
	incredible _____ _____
	independent _____ _____
	instead _____ _____
	interesting _____ _____

interrupt   _____   _____

introduce   _____   _____

5

[copy]

6

Write the words in full.

It's _____ [i–n–c–r–b–l–] how _____ [h–n–g–r–y] I was. Nevertheless, the chairman said, "I'm going to _____ [i–t–r–u–p–t–] this dinner to _____ [i–n–t–r–d–c–] an _____ [i–n–t–r–s–t–n–g] candidate who deserves your vote." I'm an _____ [i–n–d–p–d–n–t] fellow, so _____ [i–n–s–t–d] of listening, I kept on eating.

6

incredible
hungry
interrupt
introduce
interesting
independent
instead

7

Write the words in full.

Television viewers have become very _____ [i–n–d–p–n–d–t]. No longer will they watch what is merely _____ [i–n–t–r–s–t–n–g]. No, they are _____ [h–n–g–r–y] for the _____ [i–n–c–r–d–b–l–]. They listen a moment as senators _____ [i–n–t–r–d–c–] the president, but will _____ [i–n–t–r–p–t–] that program—switching channels— to look _____ [i–n–s–t–d] at an escaped monkey in a tree.

7

independent
interesting
hungry
incredible
introduce
interrupt
instead

8

PROOFREADING. Cross out any misspelled words and write the correct spelling above them.

Let me interduce myself. I am a college student with an independant mind, and am hungry for knowledge. You may think it incredable, but I find mathematics to be extremely interesting. Sometimes I inerrupt a professor's lecture with questions, insted of remaining silent.

8

introduce
independent
incredible
interrupt
instead

9

island	jealous	laboratory	language
laughter	library	lovable	

Copy each demon two times, first in print, then in handwriting. Memorize as you write.

	Print	Handwriting
island	_____	_____
jealous	_____	_____
laboratory	_____	_____
language	_____	_____
laughter	_____	_____
library	_____	_____
lovable	_____	_____

9

[copy]

10

Write the words in full.

On a distant _____ [i–l–n–d] lived a _____ [l–o–v–b–l–] girl named Gunko. Utilizing a small school _____ [l–a–b–r–t–ry] and the _____ [l–i–b–r–y], she mastered the English _____ [l–a–g–a–g–e]. Gunko's quick intelligence, her silvery _____ [l–a–t–e–r], and her tropical beauty could well make an angel _____ [j–e–l–u–s].

10

island
lovable
laboratory
library
language
laughter
jealous

11

Write the words in full.

Our _____ [l–a–n–g–a–g–] _____ [l–a–b–r–t–r–y] was like a little _____ [i–l–n–d–] in the basement of the college _____ [l–i–b–r–y]. The coeds were a bit _____ [j–e–l–u–s–] of the teacher in charge—she was always the center of happy _____ [l–a–t–r–] and so _____ [l–o–v–b–l–] it made them sick.

11

language
laboratory
island
library
jealous
laughter
lovable

12

PROOFREADING. Cross out any misspelled words and write the correct spelling above them.

Our college had a language labratory next to the libery. The woman in charge had a lovable nature, but her husband was a jelous fellow. He brooded in his private island of suspicion and resented her carefree laughter.

12

laboratory
library
jealous

13

machine	magazine	many	marriage
mathematics	maybe	meadow	

Copy each demon two times, first in print, then in handwriting. Memorize as you write.

	Print	Handwriting
machine	_____	_____
magazine	_____	_____
many	_____	_____
marriage	_____	_____
mathematics	_____	_____
maybe	_____	_____
meadow	_____	_____

13

[copy]

14

Write the words in full.

A _____ [m–a–g–z–n–] article says that _____ [m–n–y] a _____ [m–a–r–i–g–] succeeds even though both man and wife have jobs. The wife _____ [m–a–b–e–] is a professor of _____ [m–a–t–m–a–t–i–s]. Her farmer husband meanwhile sits atop a John Deere _____ [m–a–c–h–n–] and cultivates a _____ [m–e–d–o–]. Both are happy doing what they like to do.

14

magazine
many
marriage
maybe
mathematics
machine
meadow

15

Write the words in full.

Our _____ [m–a–r–i–g–e] took place in a _____ [m–e–d–o–]. [M–n–y] a flower grew there, and no gassy _____ [m–c–h–n–e] blew fumes at us. The chances of rain were _____ [m–a–b–e] one in ten, according to laws of _____ [m–a–t–h–m–t–c]—but my bride and I were lucky and happy. Our pastoral wedding was even featured in a city _____ [m–a–g–z–n–].

15

marriage
meadow
Many
machine
maybe
mathematics
magazine

16

PROOFREADING. Cross out any misspelled words and write the correct spelling above them.

I see by the cover of a supermarket magazene that another Hollywood marriage has split apart. If fat salaries can solve problems, the film actors should be as contented, maybe, as grasshoppers in a meadow. Then why do meny of them sue for divorce with such machine-like regularity? Is the fault related to egotism, not salary? The matter defies mathmatics.

16

magazine
many
mathematics

17   minute   money   muscle   necessary
             nickel   occasion   opinion

Copy each demon two times, first in print, then in handwriting. Memorize as you write.

	Print	Handwriting
minute	_____	_____
money	_____	_____
muscle	_____	_____
necessary	_____	_____
nickel	_____	_____
occasion	_____	_____
opinion	_____	_____

17

[copy]

18

Write the words in full.

Can't we earn a pile of _____ [m–n–y] without going to college? After all, didn't some dropouts with unusual _____ [m–u–s–l–] and fighting talent earn thousands of dollars per _____ [m–i–n–t–] on _____ [o–c–a–s–n–]? But the truth is that most well-paid jobs go to the fellows with education and brains. "In my _____ [o–p–i–o–n–]," says one executive, "a college education is absolutely

_____ [n–e–c–s–r–y], or your chances aren't worth a _____ [n–i–k–l–] in today's business world."

18 money muscle minute occasion opinion necessary nickel	**19** Write the words in full. I recall one unhappy _____ [o–c–a–s–n] when I stopped next to a parking meter which was hungry for _____ [m–n–y]. I had no coins, not even a _____ [n–i–k–l–]. Still, it was absolutely _____ [n–e–c–s–r–y] in my _____ [o–p–i–o–n] to have some dry-cleaning done—so I gambled. When I came out of the shop a _____ [m–i–n–t–] later, a man of _____ [m–u–s–l–] in a blue uniform was writing a citation. I was dry-cleaned again!
19 occasion money nickel necessary opinion minute muscle	**20** PROOFREADING. Cross out any misspelled words and write the correct spelling above them. Grandma brags that in the old days she could on occassion buy a hot dog for a nickel. In her opinion, George Washington threw a coin across the Delaware not only because he had muscle but because money went further in those days. But wait a minute, Grandma. When it was neccessary for you to earn money in those good old days, didn't you do babysitting for a lowly ten cents an hour?
20 occasion necessary	**21** Enter any words that you misspelled in this chapter into your Personal List of Demons in the Appendix.

REVIEW TEST: CHAPTER 13

Fill in the blanks with words studied in this chapter.

1. To win fights I need less fat and more _____ [m–u–s–l–].

2. Max sold a wooden _____ [n–i–k–l–] for ten cents.

3. Never _____ [i–n–t–r–u–p–] your boss.

4. On the porch was another _____ [m–a–g–z–n–] salesman.

5. Their _____ [m–a–r–a–g–e] lasted at least six months.

6. Bowser is a _____ [l–o–v–b–l–] dog—but he bit me.

7. Opening the aspirin bottle gave me a _____ [h–e–d–a–c–].

8. He paints _____ [i–n–t–r–s–t–g] faces, not pretty ones.

9. Robinson Crusoe landed on a sandy _____ [i–l–n–d].

10. Too bad! Your _____ [g–a–r–n–t–e] expired yesterday.

11. England decided guns are not _____ [n–e–s–r–y].

12. Baron Munchausen told _____ [i–n–c–r–b–l–] stories.

13. Pam has long teeth or _____ [m–a–b–e–] short gums.

14. Fido learned a new _____ [l–a–n–g–g–e]. He says "Moo!"

15. Othello killed his wife in a _____ [j–e–l–u–s] rage.

16. George Burns died when he was one _____ [h–u–n–d–r–d].

17. The _____ [h–n–g–r–y] cannibal had a friend for dinner.

18. Let's not confuse an _____ [o–p–i–n–n] with a fact.

19. After Hawaii, you'll find _____ [h–e–v–n] disappointing.

20. Don't shoot! I'm saving this _____ [m–n–y] for my old age.

21. The heart of a college is its _____ [l–i–b–r–y].

22. Get a job if you want to be _____ [i–n–d–p–d–n–t].

23. Check this bloodstain in the _____ [l–a–b–r–t–r–y].

24. For a baby, two plus two is higher _____ [m–a–t–m–t–c–s].

25. On one _____ [o–c–a–s–n], Sam made a U-turn in a tunnel.

KEY TO REVIEW TEST

Check your answers with the following key. Deduct 4% per error from a possible 100%.

1. muscle	**6.** lovable	**11.** necessary	**16.** hundred	**21.** library
2. nickel	**7.** headache	**12.** incredible	**17.** hungry	**22.** independent
3. interrupt	**8.** interesting	**13.** maybe	**18.** opinion	**23.** laboratory
4. magazine	**9.** island	**14.** language	**19.** heaven	**24.** mathematics
5. marriage	**10.** guarantee	**15.** jealous	**20.** money	**25.** occasion

Score: _____%

14

Capital Letters

IN THIS CHAPTER

1. a country
2. a governor
3. Algebra 1B
4. A.M.A.
5. April
6. a river
7. Atlantic Ocean
8. Buick
9. Catholics
10. Chevrolet
11. Christmas
12. December
13. Disneyland
14. drove east
15. Easter
16. Eastern oysters
17. Empire State Building
18. English
19. Father and Mother
20. flew southwest
21. Florida
22. God
23. Greek gods
24. Health Education 1A
25. history
26. his uncle
27. "Home on the Range"
28. Indians
29. *In the Midst of Life*
30. Italians
31. Jim
32. Lefty Jones
33. Lincoln
34. Magna Carta
35. Monroe Doctrine
36. Montana
37. Mr. Fudd
38. music
39. my father
40. my mother
41. Oslo
42. our high school
43. physics
44. plumbers
45. President Clinton
46. *Pride and Prejudice*
47. Republicans
48. Romeo
49. Shorty
50. Spanish
51. spring
52. Sweden
53. ten miles south
54. the Almighty
55. *The Catcher in the Rye*
56. the East
57. the Elks
58. *The Man in the Iron Mask*
59. the Middle Ages
60. the Middle East
61. the North
62. the Sierras
63. the South
64. the United Nations
65. "To the Evening Star"
66. Tuesday
67. Turkish
68. Ural Mountains
69. Wednesday
70. winter
71. World War II

COVER THIS COLUMN	1

Study the use of capital letters in the following model.

The youngest boy has become a problem. His father says, "We used to bawl him out. Now we bail him out."

a. Is the first word of each sentence capitalized? _____

b. Is the first word of a quoted sentence capitalized? _____

1

a. yes
b. yes

2

RULE: Capitalize the first word of every sentence and quoted sentence.

Insert capital letters and periods as needed.

a. my friend ate a red hot pepper his mouth was burning up then he burped and nearly set fire to the table.

b. the grave digger said, "please drop in."

c. later he went on a garlic diet soon he lost two pounds and nine friends.

d. my uncle says, "her wit is a dangerous weapon."

2

a. My
. His
. Then
b. The
Please
c. Later
. Soon
d. My
Her

3   **President Clinton   a governor**

Study the use of capital letters in the following model.

My sister once met Lefty Jones, President Clinton, Mr. Fudd, and a governor.

a. Are the names and nicknames of people capitalized? _____

b. Are the titles in front of names capitalized? _____

c. Which title is not capitalized because it is not in front of a name?

_____

3

a. yes
b. yes
c. governor

4

RULE: Capitalize names and nicknames, also the titles _____ [near/in front of] them.

4

in front of

5

Insert or cross out capital letters as necessary.

a. I wonder whether romeo really liked Juliet.

b. The theater Usher kicked shorty out of the restricted movie.

c. Our food Supervisor is captain Ptomaine.

5
 	
a. Romeo
b. usher,
   Shorty
c. supervisor,
   Captain
	6 Atlantic Ocean a river
	
	Study the use of capital letters in the following model.
	
	   Jim has crossed the Atlantic Ocean, the Ural Mountains, and a sacred river; he has girlfriends in Sweden and many a country.
	
	a. Are the specific names of places capitalized? _____
	
	b. Are *river* and *country* specific names as used in the model? _____
	
	c. Would *river* be capitalized in the name *Ohio River*? _____

6 a. yes b. no c. yes	**7** RULE: Capitalize _____ [specific/general] names of places.
7 specific	**8** Insert or cross out capital letters as necessary. a. I knew Ole could ski. He was born in oslo. b. Reuben moved to Hungry Horse, montana, and says that he likes City life. c. We swam in a few Lakes in the sierras.

8
 	
a. Oslo
b. Montana,
   city
c. lakes,
   Sierras
	9 Republicans plumbers Turkish
	
	Study the use of capital letters in the following model.
	
	   Our roving reporter interviewed Republicans, Catholics, plumbers, and Indians. He has enjoyed Italian opera, haggled in Turkish markets, and taught English classes in India.
	
	a. Are the names of specific races, nations, languages, religions, and political parties capitalized? _____
	
	b. *English* is used as an adjective in the model. Are such derivatives also capitalized? _____

9 a. yes b. yes	**10** RULE: Capitalize the names of specific races, nations, languages, and religions, _____ [but not/and also] their derivatives.

10 and also	**11** Insert or cross out capital letters as necessary. a. One gifted tramp can beg in spanish, Greek, or english. b. Even the holes in this swiss cheese cost eight cents apiece. c. In our elevator were a Caucasian, a Buddhist, and a Diabetic.

11
 	
a. Spanish,
   English
b. Swiss
c. diabetic
	12 **winter** **Christmas** **Wednesday**
	
	Study the use of capital letters in the following model.
	
	   That winter Christmas came the last Wednesday in December.
	
	a. Are the names of days, months, and holidays capitalized? _____
	
	b. Are the names of seasons capitalized? _____

12 a. yes b. no	**13** **RULE: The names of days, months, and holidays are capitalized,** _____ **[but not/and also] the names of the seasons.**
13 but not	**14** Insert or cross out capital letters as necessary. a. Those april showers hit us last tuesday. b. Sheila went to her welding class until easter that Spring.

14
 	
a. April,
   Tuesday
b. Easter,
   spring
	15 **A.M.A.** **Chevrolet** **World War II**
	
	Study the use of capital letters in the following models.
	
	   the Elks Empire State Building
	   the United Nations Chevrolet
	   A.M.A. World War II
	   Esquire Theater Magna Carta
	   our new high school the Middle Ages
	
	a. Are the names of specific organizations, historical events, periods, and documents capitalized? _____
	
	b. Is the abbreviation of an organization name capitalized? _____
	
	c. Is *high school* capitalized when it is not part of a specific name? _____

15 a. yes b. yes c. no	**16** **RULE: Capitalize the** _____ **[specific/general] names of organizations, buildings, ships, motor cars, historical events, and their abbreviations.**

16 specific	**17** Insert or cross out capital letters as necessary. a. The Monroe doctrine said, "Hands off!" b. See disneyland when you visit Florida. c. The man who built the Leaning tower of Pisa must have had one short leg. d. Millionaires have problems, too, like whether to drive the buick, the Cadillac, or the lincoln.
17 a. Doctrine b. Disneyland c. Tower d. Buick, Lincoln	**18** **Mother** **my mother** **God** **gods** Study the use of capital letters in the following models. to Father and Mother of God and His wrath to my father and my mother of the Greek gods a. Are *mother* and *father* capitalized when they are used as a name? _____ b. Are *mother* and *father* capitalized when they follow *my, our, his,* etc.? _____ c. Are references to deity capitalized? _____ d. Is *gods* (pagan) capitalized? _____
18 a. yes b. no c. yes d. no	**19** RULE: **Capitalize words that refer to deity, also *Mother* and *Father* when used as _____ [names/common nouns].**
19 names	**20** Insert or cross out capital letters as necessary. a. My aunt brought father a pot of soup. b. The almighty, our saviour, saves sinners like me. c. Pedro's Uncle prayed to the Virgin Mary.
20 a. Father b. Almighty, Saviour c. uncle	**21** **history** **Algebra 1B** Study the use of capital letters in the following model. Wanda hated history and physics, but she enjoyed Algebra 1B and Romantic Poets. a. Are specific course titles capitalized? _____ b. Are the names of general studies capitalized? _____

21 a. yes b. no	**22** **Rule: Capitalize the titles of specific courses** _____ [and/ but not] **the names of general studies.**
22 but not	**23** Insert or cross out capital letters as necessary. a. Amy needs a course in Music or biology. b. I signed for health education 1A. c. My professor in Relativity 99A was full of light and energy in his Physics lectures.

23
 	
a. music
b. Health Education
c. physics
	24 *The Catcher in the Rye*
	
	Study the use of capital letters in these models of book and song titles.
	
	    The Catcher in the Rye *Pride and Prejudice*
	    "Home on the Range" *In the Midst of Life*
	
	a. Are the first words of titles capitalized? _____
	
	b. Are the articles *(a, an, the)*, the short prepositions *(of, on, with,* etc.), and the conjunctions *(and, but, or,* etc.) usually capitalized? _____

24 a. yes b. no	**25** **Rule: Capitalize the first word and all the important words of a title, but usually not the minor articles, prepositions, and conjunctions of four letters or** _____ [more/less].
25 less	**26** Insert or cross out capital letters as necessary. a. Dumas wrote *The Man In The Iron Mask.* b. Albee wrote *Who's afraid of Virginia Woolf?* c. Wagner composed "to the Evening star."

26
 	
a. *in the*
b. *Afraid*
c. To, Star
	27 **the South** **drove east**
	
	Study the use of capitals in the following models.
	
	    ten miles south drove east
	    the South Eastern oysters
	
	a. Words that refer to specific geographical locations _____ [are/are not] capitalized.
	
	b. Words that refer to directions of the compass _____ [are/ are not] capitalized.

27 a. are b. are not	**28** **RULE: Capitalize *east, west, north, south,* etc., only when they refer to _____ [an area/a direction].**
28 an area	**29** Insert or cross out capital letters as necessary. a. We flew Southwest and visited the Middle East. b. Tex was really born in the north. c. "Go west, young man," said Horace Greeley, who lived in the east.
29 a. southwest b. North c. East	**30** Enter any words that you misspelled in this chapter into your Personal List of Demons in the Appendix.

REVIEW TEST: CHAPTER 14

Cross out any misspelling involving a capital letter and rewrite the word correctly in the space above it. If the sentence has no errors, write *OK* in front of it.

1. As a sophomore Alice drove to El Camino College in a toyota.
2. Did Mrs. Bleep give her television set to the Salvation Army?
3. Harry Lauder sang "Blue Bells Of Scotland."
4. why did Red Miller leap from the Golden Gate Bridge?
5. Don't throw garbage into lake Michigan, please.
6. Betty is studying Computers 2A and Spanish.
7. In Salem, Oregon, we saw Shakespeare's *As you Like It*.
8. By Saturday private Fleegle will be in Helsinki.
9. Last summer Emma was a baptist.
10. In Paris my uncle nearly fell off the Eiffel tower.
11. Did Olive attend a high school while in Azusa?
12. "Thank god, you're safe!" said Father Timothy.
13. Soon Captain Bragger yelled, "clean that rifle!"
14. Our State attracted German and Norwegian immigrants.
15. Joe Dingle was expelled Friday from a college in Iowa.
16. The leader of India was Mahatma Gandhi, a hindu.
17. Yes, Senator Staph, a Democrat, spoke in Bangor last Winter.
18. Germany and the Allies signed the Treaty of Versailles.
19. College freshmen like to blame their weaknesses on their high school english teachers.
20. Then Columbus sailed west and discovered the Virgin Islands.

KEY TO REVIEW TEST

Check your test answers with the following key. Deduct 5% per error from a possible 100%.

1. Toyota	**5.** Lake	**9.** Baptist	**13.** Clean	**17.** winter
2. *OK*	**6.** *OK*	**10.** Tower	**14.** state	**18.** *OK*
3. of	**7.** *You*	**11.** *OK*	**15.** *OK*	**19.** English
4. Why	**8.** Private	**12.** God	**16.** Hindu	**20.** *OK*

Score: _____ %

15

Apostrophes

IN THIS CHAPTER (partial list)

1. a day's pay
2. another's
3. anybody's
4. anyone's
5. boys and girls
6. boys' locker room
7. buzzards' nests
8. can't
9. cat's tail
10. cats' tails
11. children's choir
12. couldn't
13. Dickens' novel
14. *c*'s
15. didn't
16. doesn't
17. *8*'s
18. everybody's
19. everyone's
20. farmer's wife
21. farmers' wives
22. Francis' beard
23. girls' dormitory
24. heroes' deeds
25. hers
26. his
27. "I'll be leavin'"
28. I'm
29. "in the mornin'"
30. isn't
31. I've
32. Joe's socks
33. ladies' wigs
34. men's shorts
35. mice's tails
36. nobody's
37. o'clock
38. one's
39. *o*'s
40. ours
41. ponies' legs
42. pony's legs
43. prisoner's cell
44. someone's
45. spirit of '76
46. theirs
47. the Joneses's son
48. *3*'s
49. "wearin' nothin'"
50. women's restroom
51. you're
52. yours

COVER THIS COLUMN

1 **Joe's socks** **children's choir**

Let's see how we form the possessive of nouns that do not end in *s*.

No final *s*	Add *'s*
Joe	Joe's socks
prisoner	the prisoner's cell
women	the women's restroom
children	the children's choir

a. The nouns *Joe, prisoner, women,* and *children* _____ [do/don't] end in an *s.*

b. To form the possessive of *Joe, prisoner, women,* and *children* (nouns that do not end in an *s*), we have added _____ .

1

a. don't
b. 's

2

RULE: **If a noun does not end in *s*, we form its possessive by adding** _____ .

2

's

3

Write the possessives of these nouns that do not end in *s.*

a. dog   the ___*dog's*___ fleas

b. team   the _____ victory

c. day   a _____ pay

d. mice   _____ tails

3

b. team's
c. day's
d. mice's

4

Continue as in frame 3.

a. Bob Dylan   Bob _____ album

b. men   _____ shorts

c. mother-in-law   his _____ kitchen

d. Sears and Roebuck   Sears and _____ sale

4

a. Dylan's
b. men's
c. mother-in-law's
d. Roebuck's

5   **boys' locker room**   **Francis's beard**

Let's see how we form the possessive of nouns that already end in *s.*

Nouns ending in *s*	Add apostrophe
boys	the boys' locker room
buzzards	the buzzards' nests
Francis	Francis' beard

a. The nouns *boys, buzzards,* and *Francis* _____ [do/don't] end in *s.*

b. To form the possessive of *boys, buzzards,* and *Francis* (nouns that already end in *s*) we have added only an _____ .

5

a. do
b. '

6

RULE: **If a noun already ends in *s* we form its possessive by adding only an** _____ . (An alternate form also exists for singular nouns—for instance, *James' car* and *James's car* are both correct, but it is simpler to follow the rule as given.)

6 ,	**7** Write the possessives of these nouns that already end in *s*. a. officers the _officers'_ mess hall b. clerks the _____ strike c. Riggs _____ disease d. lovers _____ kisses e. brothers _____ quarrels
7 b. clerks' c. Riggs' d. lovers' e. brothers'	**8** Let's review how to form possessives. a. If a noun does not end in *s*, we add _____. b. If a noun does end in *s*, we add _____.
8 a. 's b. '	**9** Fill in the blanks with the correct possessive forms. a. tail of the cat = the _cat's_ tail b. tails of the cats = the _cats'_ tails c. wife of the farmer = the _____ wife d. wives of the farmers = the _____ wives
9 c. farmer's d. farmers'	**10** Continue as in frame 9. a. slums of the city = the _____ slums b. eggs of the hens = the _____ eggs c. secrets of the girls = the _____ secrets d. livers of the bulls = the _____ livers e. suits of men = _____ suits
10 a. city's b. hens' c. girls' d. bulls' e. men's	**11** Write the possessive forms. At the _____ [doctors] convention in Mexico City, I saw the surgeons remove _____ [Jose] liver and _____ [Jesus] kidney.

11 doctors' Jose's Jesus'	**12** Our rule also makes it clear that— a. boy's room = room of the boy b. boys' room = room of the _____
12 b. boys	**13** **pony's legs ponies' legs** In other words, the thing that is owned (legs) belongs to whatever comes *before* the apostrophe. Thus: a. pony's legs = legs of the _____ b. ponies' legs = legs of the _____ c. heroes' deeds = deeds of _____
13 a. pony b. ponies c. heroes	**14** **RULE: The thing that is owned (Joe's car, girls' noses) belongs to whatever comes right _____ [before/after] the apostrophe.**
14 before	**15** Apply the foregoing rule to the following phrases and *cross out* any spellings that are obviously incorrect. a. lady's wig d. mans' shoes b. ladie's wigs e. men's shoes c. ladies' wigs f. mens' shoes
15 Cross out b, d, f	**16** **one's hers** Let's see whether the indefinite pronouns and the personal pronouns form their possessives the way nouns do. INDEFINITE PRONOUNS (possessive) Right: one's, anyone's, everyone's, someone's, anybody's, everybody's, no- body's, another's PERSONAL PRONOUNS (possessive) Right: hers, his, its, ours, yours, theirs Wrong: ~~her's, our's, your's~~, etc. a. Indefinite pronouns _____ [do/don't] form possessives the way nouns do. b. Personal pronouns _____ [do/don't] form possessives the way nouns do. c. In fact, personal pronouns _____ [do/don't] use any apostrophes to show possession.

16 a. do b. don't c. don't	**17** RULE: Indefinite pronouns (*one, anybody,* etc.) form their possessives exactly like nouns. On the other hand, personal pronouns (*her, you,* etc.) ——————— [do/don't] use any apostrophes to show possession.
17 don't	**18** Write the possessive forms in full. a. the fault of somebody = *somebody's* fault b. this belongs to her = this is *hers* c. this belongs to them = this is ——————— d. crimes of nobody = ——————— crimes e. this belongs to her = this is ——————— f. this belongs to us = this is ——————— g. gift of anybody = ——————— gift h. business of someone = ——————— business
18 c. theirs d. nobody's e. hers f. ours g. anybody's h. someone's	**19** James sees and hears. . . . CAUTION: We must not get too enthusiastic and sprinkle apostrophes where they don't belong. Most words that end in *s* are not possessive at all and should not have an apostrophe. James sits on the steps and stares at the boys and girls. He sees their tricks and hears their shouts and songs as each passes by on skates. The quoted passage should have ——————— [no/two/seven] apostrophes.
19 no	**20** QUIZ Proofread the following paragraph carefully and cross out the three words that are in need of an apostrophe. Then write the correct spelling in the margin. The Astros play the Giants, and it is anybodys ball game. Little Jess, the Joneses son, sits at our television set and watches with big eyes. Between innings he hears spiels about baby-smooth shaves and matchless beers. But whose game will it be—theirs or ours? Suddenly, in the ninth, one of our sluggers blasts a low pitch over the frantic fielders and the baseball series is over—we can hear the spectators happy thunder.

20
 	
anybody's
Joneses'
spectators'
	21 isn't o'clock
	
	See how apostrophes are used to show that letters or figures are left out.
	
	    does not = doesn't you are = you're
	    is not = isn't of the clock = o'clock
	           spirit of 1776 = spirit of '76
	
	a. What letter has been left out of *isn't* and *doesn't?* _____
	
	b. The apostrophe that shows exactly where the *o* was left out of *isn't* should be placed between the letters _____ and _____.
	
	c. What does the apostrophe stand for in the historic phrase "spirit of '76"? _____

21 a. *o* b. *n, t* c. 17	**22** **RULE: An apostrophe should be placed just where letters or figures have been _____ [added/left out].**
22 left out	**23** Place apostrophes in the right places. a. dont e. doesnt b. shouldnt f. Ive run away. c. Youre handsome. g. Whos there? d. class of 93 h. Theyve gone.
23 a. don't b. shouldn't c. You're d. '93 e. doesn't f. I've g. Who's h. They've	**24** Fill in the blanks with contractions (shortened forms). They said that it (had not) _____ ever been done and that it (could not) _____ ever be done. So I (did not) _____ try.
24 hadn't couldn't didn't	**25** Continue as in frame 24. "(What is) _____ that, Madam?" asked the conductor. "(You are) _____ crying because the stranger said your baby is ugly? Come and (let us) _____ make him apologize at once. Here, (I will) _____ hold that monkey for you."

25 What's You're let's I'll	**26** **"I'll be leavin'"** See how apostrophes are sometimes used in written dialogue. "I can't stand seein' you sufferin' like that, Eliz'beth," said Smeby to his wife, "so I'll be leavin' ya' in the mornin'." a. What letter was left out of *seein'?* _____ b. What letter was left out of *Eliz'beth?* _____ c. An apostrophe can show that a sound has been _____ [added/ left out] in a spoken word.
26 a. *g* b. *a* c. left out	**27** Cross out any word that needs an apostrophe and write the correct spelling above it. "Heres a picture of me on Dads farm, feedin the pigs," said Abner. "Im the one with the hat on."
27 Here's Dad's feedin' I'm	**28** Continue as in frame 27. "I dont like answerin questions when Im wearin nothin," said Hank after the army physical examinations. "To me its embarrassin—you know what I mean?"
28 don't answerin' I'm wearin' nothin' it's embarrassin'	**29** *3's* *c's* See in the following model how we form the plural of numbers and letters. The *3's* look like *8's* on this dirty typewriter, and the *c's* look like *o's*. a. Numbers *3* and *8* were made plural by adding _____. b. Letters *c* and *o* were made plural by adding _____. c. **RULE: We add 's to make plurals of** _____ **[n–b–s] and** _____ **[l–t–s].**
29 a. *'s* b. *'s* c. numbers, letters	**30** Add apostrophes as needed. a. The Spanish don't write their *4*s and *7*s the way we do. b. Fred must learn to dot those *i*'s, cross those *t*s, and stop using those *&*s.
30 a. *4's, 7's* b. *t's, &'s*	**31** Enter any words that you misspelled in this chapter into your Personal List of Demons in the Appendix.

REVIEW TEST: CHAPTER 15

Cross out any word that needs an apostrophe and write the correct spelling above it. If the sentence has no errors, write *OK* in front of it.

1. The covers of Dickens novel are too far apart.

2. Grandpa majored in "readin and writin."

3. Toms nose runs but his feet dont.

4. Wheres the girls dormitory?

5. Whos buried in Grants tomb?

6. The Dodgers are nonviolent; they dont hit anything.

7. Gus hates to shop for his wifes underthings.

8. The Joneses car is bigger than ours.

9. Theyre kicking me out of the childrens choir.

10. If that Volvo is anybodys, its hers.

11. Lets go to Sams Delicatessen for a pastrami sandwich.

12. Doris, I cant tell your 5's from your *S*s.

13. Which rabbits are yours and which are theirs?

14. Tell me your opinions of the Finns government.

15. Dolly says shes sick of her mothers rules.

16. Do employees get coffee breaks at the Lipton Tea Company?

17. Everybodys car came in by two o clock, except yours.

18. If Julius keeps flunking, hell be in the class of 06.

19. Candidate Smeby says, "Six million Americans arent workin—even more if we count those loafin on the job."

20. Youve overheated the babys bottle.

KEY TO REVIEW TEST

Check your test answers with the following key. Deduct 3% per error from a possible 100%.

1. Dickens'
2. readin', writin'
3. Tom's, don't
4. Where's, girls'
5. Who's, Grant's
6. don't
7. wife's
8. Joneses'
9. They're, children's
10. anybody's, it's
11. Let's, Sam's
12. can't, S's
13. *OK*
14. Finns'
15. she's, mother's
16. *OK*
17. Everybody's, o'clock
18. he'll, '06
19. aren't, workin', loafin'
20. You've, baby's

Score: _____%

16

Fight Those Demons!
(106–140)

IN THIS CHAPTER

COVER THIS COLUMN

1	people	physical	pleasant	poetry
	possible	potatoes	prejudice	

Copy each demon two times, first in print, then in handwriting. Memorize as you write.

	Print	Handwriting
people	_____	_____
physical	_____	_____
pleasant	_____	_____
poetry	_____	_____
possible	_____	_____
potatoes	_____	_____
prejudice	_____	_____

1	**2**
[copy]	Write the words in full.
	_____ [P–o–t–r–y] can deal with anything—with _____ [p–e–p–l–], with _____ [p–r–j–d–i–c–], with _____ [p–o–t–a–t–s–]. The verses can be _____ [p–l–e–s–n–t–] and calming, or—yes, it is _____ [p–o–s–b–l–]—they can have an absolutely _____ [p–h–s–c–l–] effect.

2	**3**
Poetry	Write the words in full.
people	Many young _____ [p–e–p–l–] think it's _____ [p–o–s–b–l] to make a good living writing _____ [p–o–t–r–y]. Creating verses can be very _____ [p–l–s–n–t–] as a hobby, but it will rarely pay for your meat and _____ [p–t–a–t–o–s]. America cheerfully shells out millions to its heroes in _____ [p–h–s–c–l–] pursuits such as football, but it seems to entertain a blind _____ [p–r–j–d–c–] against its would-be Shakespeares.
prejudice	
potatoes	
pleasant	
possible	
physical	

3	**4**
people	PROOFREADING. Cross out any misspelled words and write the correct spelling above them.
possible	
poetry	Many people seem pleasant enough, yet it is possible that they secretly feel a
pleasant	strong predjudice against other groups. We may admire such men and
potatoes	women because they possess physical beauty or because their dancing is
physical	sheer poetry, but the truth is that such hypocrites are mighty small potatos.
prejudice	

4	**5** privilege probably professor really reason receive recommend
prejudice	Copy each demon two times, first in print, then in handwriting. Memorize as you write.
potatoes	

	Print	Handwriting
privilege	_____	_____
probably	_____	_____
professor	_____	_____
really	_____	_____

reason   _____   _____

receive   _____   _____

recommend _____   _____

5

[copy]

6

Write the words in full.

My former _____ [p–r–f–s–r–] said it was _____ [r–e–l–y] a _____ [p–r–v–l–g–] to _____ [r–e–c–m–n–d] me for the position of dog catcher. The _____ [r–e–s–n] I want that doggone job is that I'd then _____ [p–r–b–l–y] _____ [r–e–c–v–e] as good a salary as any other school dropout.

6

professor
really
privilege
recommend
reason
probably
receive

7

Write the words in full.

I _____ [r–e–c–m–n–d] that you choose a _____ [r–e–a–l–y] tough English _____ [p–r–o–f–s–r–]. The _____ [r–e–s–n–] is obvious. You have good brains and deserve to _____ [r–e–c–v–e] the best education possible. Mastering English is a _____ [p–r–i–v–l–g–e]. Some day you will _____ [p–r–o–b–l–y] thank me.

7

recommend
really
professor
reason
receive
privilege
probably

8

PROOFREADING. Cross out any misspelled words and write the correct spelling above them.

Our English proffessor will probably receive a few themes that, for no good reason, are really late. We reccomend that students be penalized for the special priviledge of submitting a late assignment.

8

professor
recommend
privilege

9   **restaurant   roommate   safety   said**
         sandwich   schedule   scissors

Copy each demon two times, first in print, then in handwriting. Memorize as you write.

	Print	Handwriting
restaurant	_____	_____
roommate	_____	_____
safety	_____	_____
said	_____	_____

sandwich	_____	_____
schedule	_____	_____
scissors	_____	_____

9

[copy]

10

Write the words in full.

My _____ [r–o–m–a–t–e], Velma, did everything on _____ [s–c–e–d–u–l–]. At noon Velma would carefully put her needles and _____ [s–i–s–e–r–s–] away—"That's for _____ [s–a–f–t–y]," she _____ [s–d]—and then she would limp to the corner _____ [r–s–t–r–a–n–t] to eat her daily tuna _____ [s–n–d–w–c–h–].

10

roommate
schedule
scissors
safety
said
restaurant
sandwich

11

Write the words in full.

My class _____ [s–c–e–d–u–l–] allowed me to work part time at the corner _____ [r–s–t–r–a–n–t]. At exactly noon my _____ [r–o–m–a–t–e], Velma, dropped in, having carefully laid away her sharp _____ [s–i–s–r–s] for _____ [s–a–f–t–y]. "Make me a tuna _____ [s–a–n–d–w–c–] this time that doesn't taste like old laundry," she _____ [s–d], "and you can give the greasy fries to a dog."

11

schedule
restaurant
roommate
scissors
safety
sandwich
said

12

PROOFREADING. Cross out any misspelled words and write the correct spelling above them.

My roomate, Velma, said she orders tuna at the corner restaraunt because

the chicken sandwich sometimes had a feather in it. Velma is also becoming

paranoid about noontime customers and plans to change her lunch sched-

ule. She has begun to carry a sharp pair of scissors to ensure her saftey.

12

roommate
restaurant
safety

---

13   secretary   separate   similar   since
        social   somebody   sophomore

Copy each demon two times, first in print, then in handwriting. Memorize as you write.

	Print	Handwriting
secretary	_____	_____
separate	_____	_____

similar _____ _____

since _____ _____

social _____ _____

somebody _____ _____

sophomore _____ _____

13

[copy]

14

Write the words in full.

For the position of _____ [s–e–c–r–t–r–y] of the _____ [s–o–p–m–r–e] class I wish to nominate _____ [s–o–m–b–d–y] with experience, namely, Jim Jones. Jim has taken part in our school's _____ [s–o–c–l–] activities _____ [s–n–c–e] he enrolled here at Guano High. Most important, he has filled _____ [s–i–m–l–r–] class offices on two _____ [s–e–p–r–t–] occasions.

14

secretary
sophomore
somebody
social
since
similar
separate

15

Write the words in full.

Does the _____ [s–o–p–m–o–r–] class of Guano High School want a truly active and talented _____ [s–o–c–l–] _____ [s–e–c–r–t–y] like Karen Krotz or just _____ [s–m–b–d–y] who can fill a position? Karen has been a dynamic leader _____ [s–n–c–e] her freshman year. Karen is intelligent, popular, sparkling—not at all _____ [s–i–m–l–r–] to that mere position-filler, Jim Jones. Let's _____ [s–e–p–r–t–e] the diamond from the imitation. Elect Karen Krotz!

15

sophomore
social
secretary
somebody
since
similar
separate

16

PROOFREADING. Cross out any misspelled words and write the correct spelling above them.

At last, the sophmore class of Guano High School will elect somebody today

to be its social secretary. Two political parties—quite similiar to each

other but separate—have formed since Jim and Karen were nominated.

Tonight one canidate will be on cloud nine; the other will be heartbroken.

16 sophomore similar candidate	**17** strictly supposed trouble truly Wednesday women writing Copy each demon two times, first in print, then in handwriting. Memorize as you write. Print Handwriting strictly _____ _____ supposed _____ _____ trouble _____ _____ truly _____ _____ Wednesday _____ _____ women _____ _____ writing _____ _____
17 [copy]	**18** Write the words in full. Freddie is _____ [t–r–l–y] in deep _____ [t–r–u–b–l–]. He's been _____ [w–r–i–t–n–g] identical love letters to two young _____ [w–m–n] back in his home town. Freddie _____ [s–u–p–o–s–] this was a safe, time-saving system, but last _____ [W–e–d–s–d–y] the two girls met and compared letters. Both are extremely angry, and for them Freddie is now _____ [s–t–r–c–l–y] off limits.
18 truly trouble writing women supposed Wednesday strictly	**19** Write the words in full. Such nerve! How could Freddie write "I love you _____ [t–r–l–y]" to two different young _____ [w–m–n]? A man is _____ [s–u–p–o–s–] to be _____ [s–t–r–c–l–y] honest when he is _____ [w–r–t–n–g] to a beloved friend. Well, Freddie's two-timing was exposed this last _____ [W–e–d–s–d–y] and Freddie is up to his big ears in terrible _____ [t–r–u–b–l–].

19

truly
women
supposed
strictly
writing
Wednesday
trouble

20

PROOFREADING. Cross out any misspelled words and write the correct spelling above them.

My English teacher says we're suppose to be in class strictly on time. But on Wednesday I had car trouble, so I arrived late. My classmates were quietly writting an impromptu theme about their most embarrassing moment. I told the teacher I was truly sorry. I knelt at his feet and kissed the floor. Some men are kind and forgiving. My teacher is not one of them.

20

supposed
writing

21

Enter any words that you misspelled in this chapter into your Personal List of Demons in the Appendix.

Fill in the blanks with words studied in this chapter.

1. A few ants will _____ [p–r–o–b–l–y] share our picnic.

2. Many a _____ [s–e–c–t–y] is smarter than her boss.

3. Sam cut his nose with his _____ [s–a–f–t–y] razor.

4. Good night and _____ [p–l–e–s–n–t] dreams!

5. My _____ [r–o–m–a–t–e] parks his boots on the sofa.

6. The sheriff and the convict had _____ [s–i–m–l–r–] backgrounds.

7. I love the _____ [p–o–t–r–y] of A. E. Housman.

8. A good judge is free of _____ [p–r–e–j–d–c–].

9. Owens was in superb _____ [p–h–s–c–l–] condition.

10. Our fullback is a meat and _____ [p–o–t–a–t–s] man.

11. The robber will _____ [r–e–c–e–v–] shiny handcuffs.

12. No, thanks, I don't want a snake _____ [s–a–n–w–i–c–].

13. To attend college is a special _____ [p–r–i–v–l–e–g–].

14. Learn to look _____ [p–e–p–l–] in the eye.

15. My druggist can't read my doctor's _____ [w–r–i–t–n–g].

16. After ten days the pair decided to _____ [s–e–p–r–a–t–].

17. Mussolini put trains back on _____ [s–c–d–u–l–].

18. It was _____ [s–u–p–o–s–] to rain today.

19. Tailors are helpless without a pair of _____ [s–i–s–r–s].

20. The ballroom was full of sweaty men and _____ [w–m–n].

21. Make _____ [s–o–m–b–d–y] happy. Mind your own business.

22. Don't enter this _____ [r–e–s–t–r–n–t] with bare feet.

23. A smart freshman becomes a _____ [s–o–p–m–o–r–].

24. The learned _____ [p–r–o–f–s–r–] swore in three languages.

25. Lucy will pitch for our team on _____ [W–e–d–s–d–y].

KEY TO REVIEW TEST

Check your test answers with the following key. Deduct 4% per error from a possible 100%.

1. probably	**6.** similar	**11.** receive	**16.** separate	**21.** somebody
2. secretary	**7.** poetry	**12.** sandwich	**17.** schedule	**22.** restaurant
3. safety	**8.** prejudice	**13.** privilege	**18.** supposed	**23.** sophomore
4. pleasant	**9.** physical	**14.** people	**19.** scissors	**24.** professor
5. roommate	**10.** potatoes	**15.** writing	**20.** women	**25.** Wednesday

Score: _____%

SUPPLEMENTARY LIST B

CHALLENGE: Study this list of troublemakers very carefully. Then—*for extra credit*—have your teacher test you on your ability to spell these eighty words correctly. Enter any misspellings into your Personal List of Demons in the Appendix.

1. accurate	**17.** diamond	**33.** lose	**49.** paralyzed	**65.** sergeant
2. acquire	**18.** dilemma	**34.** losing	**50.** poison	**66.** sincerely
3. adolescence	**19.** disastrous	**35.** maintenance	**51.** police	**67.** soldier
4. appreciate	**20.** engine	**36.** medicine	**52.** practical	**68.** souvenir
5. boundary	**21.** error	**37.** miniature	**53.** prepare	**69.** speech
6. Britain	**22.** exaggerate	**38.** mountain	**54.** procedure	**70.** stubborn
7. category	**23.** existence	**39.** mysterious	**55.** prominent	**71.** subtle
8. choose	**24.** fallacy	**40.** neutral	**56.** psychology	**72.** succeed
9. citizen	**25.** fascinate	**41.** nuisance	**57.** purchase	**73.** symbol
10. committee	**26.** future	**42.** oblige	**58.** pursue	**74.** technique
11. completely	**27.** hindrance	**43.** occurrence	**59.** quiet	**75.** travel
12. condemn	**28.** hypocrisy	**44.** ocean	**60.** rhythm	**76.** trial
13. controversy	**29.** ingredient	**45.** opportunity	**61.** rival	**77.** trousers
14. criticism	**30.** irrelevant	**46.** optimism	**62.** sailor	**78.** tyranny
15. curiosity	**31.** irresistible	**47.** pamphlet	**63.** Saturday	**79.** water
16. democracy	**32.** license	**48.** parallel	**64.** scenery	**80.** welfare

17

How Pronunciation Can Help

IN THIS CHAPTER

1. accidentally
2. Antarctic
3. Arctic
4. asked
5. athlete
6. attempt
7. candidate
8. carrying
9. congratulate
10. convenience
11. dialect
12. disgust
13. drowned
14. environment
15. equipment
16. escape
17. especially
18. everything
19. February
20. finally
21. formerly
22. government
23. grandfather
24. grievous
25. laboratory
26. length
27. liable
28. library
29. marrying
30. mischievous
31. opinion
32. practically
33. prejudiced
34. probably
35. pronuncia-
tion
36. punctuation
37. quandary
38. quantity
39. recognize
40. representa-
tive
41. similar
42. strength
43. strictly
44. studying
45. supposed to
46. surprise
47. temperament
48. temperature
49. undoubtedly
50. used to
51. valuable

COVER THIS COLUMN

1

accidentally	laboratory	temperament
dialect	liable	temperature
finally	quandary	valuable

Look closely at the letter *a* in each of the foregoing words. Notice how it affects both the pronunciation and the spelling. Now consider these two sentences:

> My microscope was finally adjusted.
> My microscope was finely adjusted.

a. Are the words *finely* and *finally* pronounced the same? _____

b. Are the two words spelled the same? _____

c. Do the two sentences have the same meaning? _____

1

a. no
b. no
c. no

2

Observe that *liable* (li–a–ble) has three syllables, not two. *Temperature* (tem–per–a–ture) has four syllables, not three. People who skip a syllable in their pronunciation are as a result _____ [more/less] likely to skip a letter in their spelling.

2

more

3

How many syllables do the following words have? You may consult your dictionary if you wish.

a. accidentally _*five*_   d. quandary   _____

b. dialect   _____   e. temperament   _____

c. finally   _____   f. valuable   _____

3

b. three
c. three
d. three
e. four
f. four

4

Pronounce each word ten times, emphasizing the sound of the capitalized letter. Then write the word three times, capitalizing the key letter to help you remember it.

accidentAlly   *accidentAlly*   _____   _____

diAlect   _____   _____   _____

finAlly   _____   _____   _____

laborAtory   _____   _____   _____

liAble   _____   _____   _____

quandAry   _____   _____   _____

temperAment   _____   _____   _____

temperAture   _____   _____   _____

valuAble   _____   _____   _____

4

[copy]

5   **QUIZ**

Write the words in full.

In chemistry _____ [lab–ty] I spilled acids at high _____ [temp–re]. Then I used a _____ [val–ble] barometer and _____ [accid–ly] broke it. I was in a _____ [quan–ry]. Professor Blatz in his foreign _____ [d–lect] suggested that I ought to major in folk dancing, so I _____ [fin–ly] left.

5 laboratory temperature valuable accidentally quandary dialect finally	**6** **probably** **Arctic** **punctuation** **Antarctic** **practically** Some people forget to pronounce the letter *c* in *ct* combinations. Which of the foregoing words may give them trouble? _____ _____ _____ _____
6 Arctic Antarctic practically punctuation	**7** Pronounce each word ten times; then write each word three times, including the capital letters. proBaBly *proBaBly* _____ _____ Arctic _____ _____ _____ Antarctic _____ _____ _____ practically _____ _____ _____ punctuation _____ _____ _____

7
 	
[copy]
	8
	
	Write the words in full.
	
	a. Themes deserve good _____ [pun–tion].
	
	b. The forecast is that it will _____ [prob–] be sunny—so it will
	
	    _____ [prob–] rain.
	
	c. "Cold-Feet" Mulligan hiked through _____ [pra–c–ly] the whole
	
	    _____ [Ar–ic] and _____ [Ant–r–ic].

8
 	
a. punctuation
b. probably,
    probably
c. practically,
    Arctic,
    Antarctic
	9 **asked** **grandfather** **supposed to** **used to**
	        candidate **prejudiced** **undoubtedly**
	
	An angry professor once threatened to break a ruler over the head of any student who omitted the letter *d* when it belonged at the end of a word. If you were in his class, which four words in the following statement would you pronounce and spell rather carefully? Circle them.
	
	"Simon was supposed to be a big shot, and students used to think he was prejudiced, too—but he often asked me to share a salami sandwich."

9

supposed
used
prejudiced
asked

10

Pronounce each word ten times; then write each word three times, including the capital letters.

askeD   _askeD_   _____   _____

canDidate   _____   _____   _____

granDfather   _____   _____   _____

prejudiceD   _____   _____   _____

supposeD to   _____   _____   _____

undoubteDly   _____   _____   _____

useD to   _____   _____   _____

10

[copy]

11

"Prejudice is an evil thing. Are you prejudiced?" Notice that the adjective *prejudiced* ends with the letter _____ . Fill in the blanks that follow.

a. I'd be a Beauty Queen, but the judges are _____ [prej–].

b. Teacher is _____ [prej–]—against laziness.

11

d
a. prejudiced
b. prejudiced

12

Fill in the blanks.

a. That beggar _____ [us–] to be a banker.

b. I was _____ [suppos–] to bunt.

c. The customer had _____ [ask–] for baloney.

12

a. used
b. supposed
c. asked

---

13   **QUIZ**

Write the words in full.

My _____ [gra–father] was a _____ [can–date] for city clerk. He _____ [ask–] everybody to vote for him and he _____ [suppos–] he'd _____ [undoubt–ly] win. But he lost the election and later _____ [us–] to tell us the voters were all _____ [prej–].

13

grandfather
candidate
asked
supposed
undoubtedly
used
prejudiced

---

14   disgust   length   recognize   strength

a. Some folks will talk about the "len'th" of a road or the "stren'th" of a mule. If they realized that *length* and *strength* are related to *long* and *strong*, they would be more sure to pronounce the letter_____.

b. *Recognize* comes from the same Latin root as *cognition, cognizant,* and *incognito.* Which four letters, found in all these words, are Latin for "know"? _____

14

a. *g*
b. *cogn*

15

Pronounce each word ten times; then write each word three times, including the capital letters.

disGust   *disGust*   _____   _____

lenGth   _____   _____   _____

recoGnize   _____   _____   _____

strenGth   _____   _____   _____

15

[copy]

---

16   QUIZ

Write the words in full.

I hoped our coach would _____ [rec–ze] my great _____ [str–th]. I threw the discus a _____ [le–th] of twelve feet, then gave up in _____ [dis–st].

16

recognize
strength
length
disgust

---

17   convenience   environment   government   opinion

Big words often have little words inside of them. Look for these little words—sometimes they can help your pronunciation and spelling.

a. What metal do you see in *environment?* _____

b. What nickname do you see in *government?* _____

c. What sharp object do you see in *opinion?* _____

17

a. iron
b. Vern
c. pin

18

Pronounce each word distinctly ten times; then write it three times, including the capital letters.

conveNience   *conveNience*   _____   _____

enviRONment   _____   _____   _____

goVERNment   _____   _____   _____

oPINion   _____   _____   _____

18

[copy]

19

Write the words in full.

a. Notice the *iron* in our _____ [env–ment].

b. Vern runs our _____ [gov–ment].

c. Las Vegas tries to give conventions every _____ [conv–nce].

d. Who gives a pin for Ben's _____ [op–n]?

19

a. environment
b. government
c. convenience
d. opinion

---

20 February formerly library surprise

Consider the sentence: "Mayor Klutz [formally/formerly] welcomed the rock bands." Which consonant would you pronounce distinctly if you meant "at an earlier time"? _____

20

r

21

Pronounce each word ten times; then write each word three times, including the capital letters.

FebRuary   *FebRuary* _____   _____

formeRly   _____   _____   _____

libRary   _____   _____   _____

suRprise   _____   _____   _____

21

[copy]

22

Write the words in full.

What a pleasant _____ [s–pse] to see your son in the _____ [lib–ry] this _____ [Feb–y]! He _____ [form–ly] did his sleeping on the grass.

22

surprise
library
February
formerly

---

23 escape especially

Pronounce each word ten times; then write each word three times, including the capital letters.

escape   *eScape* _____   _____

especially   _____   _____   _____

23

[copy]

24

Write the words in full.

Bugsy wanted to _____ [e–c–pe] and go home, _____ [e–pec–ly] because it was Mother's Day. But he was persuaded not to _____ [e–c–pe]. Guns were _____ [e–pec–ly] convincing.

---

24 escape especially escape especially	**25** attempt quantity strictly congratulate representative Careless speakers and writers sometimes forget the *t* when it follows a consonant. a. What four-letter word is in the middle of *representative?* _____ b. What five-letter word is at the end of *attempt?* _____
25 a. *sent* b. *tempt*	**26** Pronounce each word ten times; then write each word two times, including the capital letters. attempT *attempT*_____ _____ congraTulate _____ _____ quanTity _____ _____ represenTative _____ _____ stricTly _____ _____
26 [copy]	**27** Write the words in full. Lady, I'm a sales _____ [rep–s–tive], and I _____ [c–gr–late] you on winning a toothbrush. I'll now _____ [attem–] to sell you a _____ [qu–n–ty] of products. Terms are _____ [stri–ly] cash.
27 representative congratulate attempt quantity strictly	**28** carrying everything marrying studying When *ing* is added to *carry, marry,* and *study,* the *y* is _____ [kept/dropped]. Repeat the word *studying* until you can hear the *y*.
28 kept	**29** Pronounce each word ten times; then write each word three times, including the capital letters. carrYing *carrYing*_____ _____ everYthing _____ _____ _____ marrYing _____ _____ _____

29

[copy]

30

Write the words in full.

Al is ＿＿＿＿＿＿ [stud–g] to be a goat farmer. He is now ＿＿＿＿＿＿ [carr–g] books about goats to his sweetheart. "If ＿＿＿＿＿＿ [ev–thing] goes well," says Al, "we'll be ＿＿＿＿＿＿ [marr–g] soon and raising kids."

30

studying
carrying
everything
marrying

---

31 THE NO-EXTRA-LETTERS-PLEASE GANG

athlete	equipment	mischievous	similar
drowned	grievous	pronunciation	

Examine these words—they are dangerous. If we collected a penny each time some careless speller put an extra letter into one of these words, we could ride on gold bicycles. But pronounce these words right and you'll spell them right.

What letter comes after—

a. the *th* in *athlete?* ＿＿＿＿＿＿

b. the *n* in *drowned?* ＿＿＿＿＿＿

c. the *p* in *equipment?* ＿＿＿＿＿＿

d. the *v* in *grievous?* ＿＿＿＿＿＿

e. the *v* in *mischievous?* ＿＿＿＿＿＿

f. the *pron* in *pronunciation?* ＿＿＿＿＿＿

g. the *l* in *similar?* ＿＿＿＿＿＿

31

a. *l*
b. *e*
c. *m*
d. *o*
e. *o*
f. *u*
g. *a*

32

Pronounce each word ten times; then write each word three times—and add no extra letters, please.

athlete ＿＿＿＿＿ ＿＿＿＿＿ ＿＿＿＿＿

drowned ＿＿＿＿＿ ＿＿＿＿＿ ＿＿＿＿＿

equipment ＿＿＿＿＿ ＿＿＿＿＿ ＿＿＿＿＿

grievous ＿＿＿＿＿ ＿＿＿＿＿ ＿＿＿＿＿

mischievous ＿＿＿＿＿ ＿＿＿＿＿ ＿＿＿＿＿

pronunciation ＿＿＿＿＿ ＿＿＿＿＿ ＿＿＿＿＿

similar ＿＿＿＿＿ ＿＿＿＿＿ ＿＿＿＿＿

32

[copy]

---

33 QUIZ

Write the words in full.

An _____ [ath–te] in football _____ [equ–ment] ran smack

into the swimming pool, a _____ [gr–v–us] blunder. He nearly

_____ [drown–]. You see, our doors all look _____ [sim–l–r],

and a _____ [misch–s] boy had left the wrong door open. The

waterlogged _____ [ath–te] came up swearing—and with what

_____ [pron–c–tion]!

33

athlete
equipment
grievous
drowned
similar
mischievous
athlete
pronunciation

34

Enter any words that you misspelled in this chapter into your Personal
List of Demons in the Appendix.

REVIEW TEST: CHAPTER 17

Fill in the blanks with words studied in this chapter.

1. My brain surgeon was _____ [prob–y] a veterinarian.

2. The plumber forgot to bring his _____ [equip–t].

3. Mother stuck _____ [str–c–ly] to her diet and gained a pound.

4. Meeting my parole officer was a pleasant _____ [s–pr–se].

5. Salesman Sam could sell bikinis in the _____ [Ar–ic].

6. I froze my ears last _____ [Feb–ry].

7. Mr. Scrooge _____ [fin–ly] spent fifteen cents.

8. A sentence must end with some kind of _____ [pu–t–ation].

9. Joe found books and girls in the _____ [lib–ry].

10. Slim had a narrow _____ [e–cape].

11. Use a dictionary to check _____ [pron–n–a–on].

12. Radioactive wastes do not improve our _____ [env–r–ment].

13. A polar bear in this _____ [temp–t–re] would build a fire.

14. Nan can outrun me, _____ [car–ing] two buckets of sand.

15. People vote for the most promising _____ [can–date].

16. I smelled bad eggs in the _____ [lab–t–ry].

17. Many a female _____ [ath–te] has run the marathon.

18. Pete _____ [form–ly] pitched for the Hoboken Hoboes.

19. You aren't _____ [sup–os–] to listen with your mouth.

20. Rusty had taken iron tablets to build up his _____ [stre–th].

21. Healthy Harry drank a _____ [quan–ty] of carrot juice.

22. Can you _____ [rec–g–ze] the man who mugged you?

23. Otto _____ [ac–d–nt–ly] fell into the huge sausage grinder.

24. Our gymnasium was sixty feet in _____ [l–n–t–].

25. My _____ [gr–father] used to spank my father.

26. Hiking through the poison ivy was a _____ [gr–v–us] mistake.

27. Losers usually claim that the umpire is _____ [pr–jud–].

28. Gwendolyn is _____ [st–d–ng] to be an architect.

29. Buy a car now and get a _____ [val–bl–] ball-point pen.

30. Slobbovia had a brand-new _____ [gov–m–nt] every six months.

31. Mrs. Clemens _____ [drow–d] the kittens in warm water.

32. Memorize _____ [ev–thing] in this fat book.

33. Abe Lincoln _____ [us–] to write on a shovel.

KEY TO REVIEW TEST

Check your test answers with the following key. Deduct 3% per error from a possible 100%.

1. probably
2. equipment
3. strictly
4. surprise
5. Arctic
6. February
7. finally

8. punctuation
9. library
10. escape
11. pronunciation
12. environment
13. temperature
14. carrying

15. candidate
16. laboratory
17. athlete
18. formerly
19. supposed
20. strength
21. quantity

22. recognize
23. accidentally
24. length
25. grandfather
26. grievous
27. prejudiced
28. studying

29. valuable
30. government
31. drowned
32. everything
33. used

Score: _____ %

SUPPLEMENTARY LIST C

Spelling gimmicks: A gimmick is a tricky phrase or device that helps you remember how to spell a word.

Study the following spelling words and gimmicks carefully. Memorize gimmicks only for words that keep giving you trouble.

Make up your own gimmicks when necessary. Keep them short. Record them in your Personal List of Demons in the Appendix.

Exercise: On a separate piece of paper (a) copy each gimmick in the following list, and (b) use the word correctly in a short sentence of your own.

Then—*for extra credit*—have your teacher test you on your ability to spell these words.

1. accommodate: acCOMMOdate COMMON people
2. acquainted: ACquainted with AC current
3. across: see A CROSS ACROSS the street
4. advice: advICE about ICE
5. advise: WISE men advISE
6. all right: ALL wrong; ALL right
7. apparently: apPARENTly she's the PARENT
8. approach: appROACH the ROACH
9. argument: arGUMent over GUM
10. balloon: BALLoon like a BALL
11. beginning: begINNING of an INNING
12. benefited: see VAC rule (chap. 12)

13. berth: BErth is a BEd

14. blouse: a LOUSE on the bLOUSE

15. bulletin: a BULLET IN a BULLETIN

16. business: use a BUS IN BUSINESS

17. calendar: calenDAR of the D.A.R.

18. candidate: my canDIDate DID win

19. capitol: capitol dome

20. cemetery: E-E-E! it's the cEMETEry!

21. choose: fOOls chOOse bOOze

22. chose: she chOSE a rOSE

23. criticism: CRITICism begins with a CRITIC

24. customer: a CUSTOMer has a CUSTOM

25. desperate: a despERAte ERA

26. dictionary: NARY a dictioNARY

27. dilemma: the dilEMMA of EMMA

28. divine: DIVINE DIVINg

29. dormitory: dorMITory at M.I.T.

30. eighth: EIGHT + H = EIGHTH

31. environment: IRON in envIRONment

32. excellent: exCELLent CELL

33. exhilarate: HILARity exHILARates

34. existence: TEN years of exisTENce

35. explanation: PLAN your exPLANation

36. familiar: a famiLIAR LIAR

37. February: BR! FeBRuary is cold

38. forty: spORTy at fORTy

39. gasoline: gasoLINE LINE

40. ghost: our HOST is a gHOST

41. government: VERN runs our goVERNment

42. grammar: we often MAR grammAR

43. grease: EASE work with grEASE

44. height: H + EIGHT = HEIGHT

45. hundred: hundRED RED men

46. hypocrisy: CRISis of hypoCRISy

47. independent: indepenDENT DENT

48. irrelevant: Oscar LEVANT was irreLEVANT

49. laundry: DRY launDRY

50. led: TED was lED to bED

51. librarian: liBRArian wore a BRA

52. literature: earn A in literATure

53. loose: lOOse gOOse

54. merchant: CHANT of the merCHANT

55. modern: MODErn MODE

56. monarchy: ARCHY runs a monARCHY

57. morale: ALE ends morALE

58. municipal: municiPAL PAL

59. mustache: MUSTACHE MUST ACHE

60. necessary: only one C is neCessary

61. nickel: nickEL to ride the EL

62. occasion: occaSION of the invaSION

63. optimistic: TIM IS opTIMIStic

64. original: GINA is oriGINAl

65. pamphlet: PAM wrote a PAMphlet

66. parallel: ALL EL tracks are parALLEL

67. parliament: I AM in parlIAMent

68. passion: PASSion will PASS

69. peculiar: pecuLIAR LIAR

70. picnicking: I'm PICNIC KING

71. piece: PIEce of PIE

72. potatoes: potaTOES have TOES

73. practical: practiCAL CAL

74. prejudice: PREJUDge; PREJUDice

75. principle: principLE ruLE

76. privilege: special priVILEge is VILE

77. professor: proFESSOR and conFESSOR

78. receive: *i* before *e,* except after *c*

79. referred: see VAC rule (chap. 12)

80. remember: a MEMBER will reMEMBER

81. repetition: PETITION for rePETITION

82. restaurant: AURA of a restAURAnt

83. schedule: YULE schedULE

84. separate: PAR on sePARAte golf courses

85. sergeant: SERGEant wore SERGE

86. stationery: stationERY is papER

87. steak: TEA and STEAK

88. stomach: ACH, my stomACH

89. tenant: NAN is a teNANt

90. they're: THEY'RE = THEY aRE

91. tongue: LONG tonGue

92. tragedy: tRAGEdy was the RAGE

93. translate: transLATE on the SLATE

94. truly: it's trULy JULY

95. twelfth: twELFth ELF

96. villain: VILLAin has a VILLA

97. who's: WHO'S = WHO iS

98. woman: MAN and woMAN

99. women: MEN and woMEN

100. you're: YOU'RE = YOU aRE

18

Words with Tricky Endings

IN THIS CHAPTER

COVER THIS COLUMN

1   comfortable   horrible

Examine carefully the roots to which we add *able* and the roots to which we add *ible*.

able		ible	
acceptable	excusable	audible	permissible
advisable	fashionable	divisible	possible
considerable	laughable	edible	terrible
comfortable	receivable	eligible	visible
debatable	suitable	feasible	
dependable	valuable	horrible	
desirable		incredible	

197

a. **RULE: If the root is a full word—for example, *accept*, *comfort*, *fashion*—we usually add _____ [*able*/*ible*].**

b. **RULE: If the root is not a full word—for example, *aud*, *ed*, *horr*, *terr*—we usually add _____ [*able*/*ible*].**

1

a. *able*
b. *ible*

2

a. The root *suit* is a full word, so we add _____.

b. The root *vis* is not a full word, so we add _____.

2

a. *able*
b. *ible*

3

Fill in the blanks as shown. If the root is a full word add *able*; otherwise, add *ible*.

accept	*acceptable*	_____	_____
aud	_____	_____	_____
comfort	_____	_____	_____
consider	_____	_____	_____
vis	_____	_____	_____
elig	_____	_____	_____

3

audible
comfortable
considerable
visible
eligible

4

We usually add *able* to a root that is a _____ [full/incomplete] word.

4

full

5

The root *terr* is not a full word, so we give it what ending? _____ [*able*/*ible*]

5

ible

6

Write the words in full, adding *able* or *ible*.

fashion	*fashionable*	suit	_____
divis	_____	laugh	_____
poss	_____	incred	_____

| 6 | 7 excusable valuable |

6

divisible
possible
suitable
laughable
incredible

---

7 excusable valuable

But suppose the root is a full word that ends in *e*:

$$\text{excuse} + \text{able} = \text{excusable}$$
$$\text{value} + \text{able} = \text{valuable}$$

RULE: When *able* is added to a word like *excuse* or *value* that ends in *e*, the *e* is _____ [kept/dropped].

7

dropped

---

8 advisable

Fill in the blanks as shown. Note that the roots are full words ending in *e*, and that you must drop the *e* before adding *able*.

advise   *advisable*   _____   _____

debate   _____   _____   _____

desire   _____   _____   _____

excuse   _____   _____   _____

receive _____   _____   _____

8

debatable
desirable
excusable
receivable

9

Let's review the BASIC RULES for adding *able* or *ible*.

a. **When the root is a complete word—for example, *depend*, *perish*, *profit*, or *remark*—we usually add _____ .**

b. **When the root is a complete word that ends in *e*—for example, *deplore*, *describe*, or *excuse*—we drop the letter _____ and then add _____ .**

c. **When the root is not a complete word—for example, *divis*, *permiss*, *feas*, *dirig*, or *incred*—we usually add _____ .**

9

a. *able*
b. *e, able*
c. *ible*

10

Fill in the blanks with words ending in *able* or *ible*.

a. A secretary must be _____ [depend–].

b. Athletes study to stay _____ [elig–].

c. A tunnel to France? Is it _____ [feas–]?

d. Gambling in church isn't _____ [excuse].

10 a. dependable b. eligible c. feasible d. excusable	**11** Continue as in frame 10. a. If Fido lives, the mushrooms are _____ [ed–]. b. Our sins are _____ [consider–]. c. Grandma's sweatshirt isn't _____ [suit–]. d. The best of wars is _____ [horr–].
11 a. edible b. considerable c. suitable d. horrible	**12** Continue as in frame 10. a. Skinny's appetite is _____ [incred–]. b. Whether humankind can survive is _____ [debate]. c. His trunks fell off. How _____ [laugh–]! d. Smoking in class isn't _____ [permiss–].
12 a. incredible b. debatable c. laughable d. permissible	**13** probable digestible responsible EXCEPTIONS. Now let's study a few—darn it!—exceptions. Try to see why each of the following spellings is an exception to our rule. irritable *irritable* _____ _____ inevitable _____ _____ _____ probable _____ _____ _____ contemptible _____ _____ _____ digestible _____ _____ _____ flexible _____ _____ _____ responsible _____ _____ _____ a. Note that *irrit, inevit,* and *prob* are *not* complete words; yet they take what ending? _____ b. Note that *contempt, digest, flex,* and *response* are complete words, yet take what ending? _____ c. Write each word three times in the spaces provided.
13 a. *able* b. *ible* c. [copy]	**14** **QUIZ ON EXCEPTIONS** Write the words in full. a. Raw fish can be _____ [digest–]. b. Vandals are _____ [contempt–]. c. Stalled traffic makes me _____ [irrit–].

d. Smash-ups are not _____ [inevit–].

e. That idiotic driver is _____ [response].

f. The gossip's tongue is _____ [flex–].

g. An atomic war is _____ [prob–].

14

a. digestible
b. contemptible
c. irritable
d. inevitable
e. responsible
f. flexible
g. probable

15　　　　-er　　　　-or　　　　-ar

Deciding whether a word ends in *er, or,* or *ar* can be a thorn in the student's anatomy.

The ending *er* is extremely common (*father, writer, driver,* etc.); the ending *or* is less common than *er* and it suggests a Latin origin (*benefactor, professor, doctor, senator,* etc.); the ending *ar* is unusual and sneaky (*calendar, particular, similar,* etc.).

If in despair as to whether a word ends in *er, or,* or *ar,* you should solve the problem by means of a _____ [guess/dictionary].

15

dictionary

16　　　　**teacher**

The ending *er* often means "one who does."

He who teaches is a *teacher;* he who paints is a _____; he who bakes is a _____ .

16

painter
baker

17

To change a verb like *paint* or *bake* into a noun like *painter* or *baker,* we usually give it the ending _____ .

17

er

18　　　　**speaker**

Write nouns that mean "one who does."

a. speak, *speaker*   e. employ, _____

b. play, _____   f. murder, _____

c. pitch, _____   g. accuse, _____

d. advertise, _____   h. stink, _____

18

b. player
c. pitcher
d. advertiser
e. employer
f. murderer
g. accuser
h. stinker

19　　　　**benefactor**　　**humor**　　　**motor**
　　　　　　　doctor　　　　**inventor**　**senator**
　　　　　　　governor　　**labor**　　　**sponsor**

a. Pronounce each of the *or* words several times, exaggerating slightly (but only to yourself) the sound of the *o* in the endings. Learning these *or* words involves a little labOR.

b. Write each word three times, capitalizing the letter o as shown.

benefactor   *benefactOr*   _____   _____

doctor   _____   _____   _____

governor   _____   _____   _____

humor   _____   _____   _____

inventor   _____   _____   _____

labor   _____   _____   _____

motor   _____   _____   _____

senator   _____   _____   _____

sponsor   _____   _____   _____

19

b. [copy]

20

Write the words in full.

Consider the _____ [invent–] of the first _____ [mot–] car.
Was he a _____ [benef–] of _____ [lab–], or did he just have a
nasty sense of _____ [hum–]? Recently, a _____ [doct–] persuaded his _____ [senat–] and his _____ [gov–] to _____
[spons–] yet another bill to control automobile fumes.

20

inventor
motor
benefactor
labor
humor
doctor
senator
governor
sponsor

21

Write the words in full.

a. "Take two aspirins," said the _____ [doc–].

b. I voted for a fairly honest _____ [senat–].

c. Let's _____ [spons–] education, not war.

d. If my automobile _____ [mot–] were a man, he'd be ninety
years old.

e. In the taxi, Flo got _____ [lab–] pains.

f. The monkey bit its _____ [benefact–].

g. Every _____ [gov–] wants to be president.

h. Now, Mr. Piltdown, you say—ha, ha!—that you are the _____
[invent–] of a wheel?

i. Will Rogers wrote a _____ [hum–] column.

21

a. doctor
b. senator
c. sponsor
d. motor
e. labor
f. benefactor
g. governor
h. inventor
i. humor

22

beggar	calendar	scholar
burglar	particular	similar

a. The words listed in this frame need particulAR attention because they all end in _____ .

b. Pronounce each word several times, exaggerating slightly (but only to yourself) the sound of the *a* in the endings.

c. Write each word three times, capitalizing the letter *a* as shown.

beggAR   *beggAr* _____ _____

burglAR _____ _____ _____

calendAR _____ _____ _____

particulAR _____ _____ _____

scholAR _____ _____ _____

22

a. *ar*
b. [copy]

23

Write the words in full.

Once a _____ [burg–] searched the home of a _____ [sch–], but all he could steal was a _____ [cal–]. A _____ [beg–] had _____ [sim–] luck—he got a free lecture on private enterprise, which did him no _____ [partic–] good since he was already practicing it in his own way.

23

burglar
scholar
calendar
beggar
similar
particular

24

Write the words in full.

a. The twins are as _____ [sim–] as beans.

b. The _____ [beg–] had a roll of twenties.

c. Order stew, if you're not _____ [partic–].

d. See the cute cat on every _____ [cal–].

e. The _____ [sch–] finally added a footnote.

24

a. similar
b. beggar
c. particular
d. calendar
e. scholar

---

25   **QUIZ**

Write words that end in *er, or,* or *ar*.

a. [simil–] _____   f. [hum–] _____

b. [mot–] _____   g. [foreign–] _____

c. [weath–] _____   h. [spons–] _____

d. [doct–] _____   i. [listen–] _____

c. [calend–] _____   j. [partic–] _____

25

a. similar
b. motor
c. weather
d. doctor
e. calendar
f. humor
g. foreigner
h. sponsor
i. listener
j. particular

26

Enter any words that you misspelled in this chapter into your Personal List of Demons in the Appendix.

Fill in the blanks with words that end in *able* or *ible*.

1. The power of gossip is _____ [incred–].

2. Your spiked heels aren't _____ [suit–] for hiking.

3. Locking a dog in a hot car is _____ [contempt–].

4. My value to the team was _____ [debate].

5. Ability to spell is extremely _____ [value].

6. Grandpa's snoring was _____ [aud–].

7. She loves me! Is it _____ [poss–]?

8. A bridge to the moon isn't _____ [feas–].

9. That beagle has _____ [remark–] ears.

10. Water beds are _____ [comfort–].

11. Our nation is one and _____ [indivis–].

12. When Bobo drives, a crash is _____ [inevit–].

13. He's no doctor. His writing is _____ [leg–].

14. One bloody czar was named Ivan the _____ [Terr–].

15. The tiger decided I wouldn't be _____ [digest–].

Fill in the blanks with words that end in *er, or,* or *ar.*

16. My old car needs a _____ [mot–] transplant.

17. All rats look quite _____ [simi–].

18. My _____ [doct–] dislikes being around sick people.

19. Scribble your appointments on a _____ [calend–].

20. The paint store _____ [burgl–] was caught red-handed.

21. This _____ [advertis–] speaks with forked tongue.

22. When TV programs are bad, complain to the _____ [spons–].

23. Fanatics lose their sense of _____ [hum–].

24. The _____ [beg–] was a strolling winery.

25. Melville is the _____ [auth–] of *Moby Dick*.

KEY TO REVIEW TEST

Check your test answers with the following key. Deduct 4% per error from a possible 100%.

1. incredible	6. audible	11. indivisible	16. motor	21. advertiser
2. suitable	7. possible	12. inevitable	17. similar	22. sponsor
3. contemptible	8. feasible	13. legible	18. doctor	23. humor
4. debatable	9. remarkable	14. Terrible	19. calendar	24. beggar
5. valuable	10. comfortable	15. digestible	20. burglar	25. author

Score: _____ %

SUPPLEMENTARY LIST D

Study List D very carefully. Then—for extra credit—have your teacher test you on your mastery of these words with tricky endings.

Here note in particular the ending—*able* or *ible*.

1. adorable	7. enviable	13. perishable	19. remarkable	25. perfectible
2. available	8. excitable	14. personable	20. taxable	26. plausible
3. breakable	9. expandable	15. predictable	21. combustible	27. reversible
4. creditable	10. indescribable	16. presentable	22. compatible	28. sensible
5. deplorable	11. memorable	17. profitable	23. convertible	29. susceptible
6. detestable	12. peaceable	18. reliable	24. indelible	30. tangible

Note in particular the ending—*ar, er,* or *or.*

1. cellar	6. spectacular	11. foreigner	16. commentator	21. orator
2. lunar	7. accuser	12. listener	17. conductor	22. radiator
3. nuclear	8. advertiser	13. maneuver	18. contributor	23. spectator
4. pillar	9. consumer	14. ancestor	19. counselor	24. survivor
5. polar	10. debater	15. aviator	20. elevator	25. visitor

Appendix

PERSONAL LIST OF DEMONS

Keep a list here of any words in this manual or in your English compositions that keep giving you spelling trouble.

a. Write each word correctly five times; then use it in a sentence. Add a gimmick (memory aid) if you can think of one. Example:

> **17.** argument argument argument argument argument
> Ringo and I had an argument [arGUMent over GUM]

b. Review this personal list of demons at least once a week.

c. Have a student or teacher test you on your mastery of these demons.

1. _____

_____

2. _____

_____

3. _____

_____

_____

_____

_____

_____

_____

_____

_____

_____

_____

_____

_____

_____

_____

_____

_____

_____

_____

_____

_____

_____

_____

_____

_____

_____

_____

_____

_____

_____

_____

_____

_____

_____

_____

ANALYSIS OF SPELLING ERRORS

Some students tend to make particular kinds of errors. They have an unhappy talent for leaving letters out or for turning letters around or, perhaps, for mixing up homonyms (sound-alikes). Yet if they knew their favorite faults, they could be on their guard against them. Knowing a special weakness is half the battle.

Analyze your own personal demons. Find out whether your errors have been due mainly to (I) homonyms, (II) capital letters, (III) apostrophes, (IV) noun plurals, (V) missing letters, (VI) extra letters, (VII) wrong letters, (VIII) reversed letters, (IX) penmanship, or (X) miscellaneous.

In the appropriate spaces, list the words that you have misspelled, according to the nature of the errors that you made. That is, write the word correctly in the group where it belongs.

I. HOMONYMS (for example, *their*—spelled by error like *there*)

1. _____ 6. _____ 11. _____
2. _____ 7. _____ 12. _____
3. _____ 8. _____ 13. _____
4. _____ 9. _____ 14. _____
5. _____ 10. _____ 15. _____

II. CAPITAL LETTERS (for example, *English*—spelled by error with a small *e*)

1. _____ 6. _____ 11. _____
2. _____ 7. _____ 12. _____
3. _____ 8. _____ 13. _____
4. _____ 9. _____ 14. _____
5. _____ 10. _____ 15. _____

III. APOSTROPHES (for example, *says*—spelled by error with an apostrophe)

1. _____ 6. _____ 11. _____
2. _____ 7. _____ 12. _____
3. _____ 8. _____ 13. _____
4. _____ 9. _____ 14. _____
5. _____ 10. _____ 15. _____

IV. NOUN PLURALS (for example, *enemies*—spelled by error with a *y*)

1. _____ 6. _____ 11. _____
2. _____ 7. _____ 12. _____
3. _____ 8. _____ 13. _____
4. _____ 9. _____ 14. _____
5. _____ 10. _____ 15. _____

V. MISSING LETTERS (for example, *studying*—spelled by error without the *y*)

1. _____	6. _____	11. _____
2. _____	7. _____	12. _____
3. _____	8. _____	13. _____
4. _____	9. _____	14. _____
5. _____	10. _____	15. _____

VI. EXTRA LETTERS (for example, *writing*—spelled by error with an extra *t*)

1. _____	6. _____	11. _____
2. _____	7. _____	12. _____
3. _____	8. _____	13. _____
4. _____	9. _____	14. _____
5. _____	10. _____	15. _____

VII. WRONG LETTERS (for example, *escape*—spelled by error with an *x* instead of an *s*)

1. _____	6. _____	11. _____
2. _____	7. _____	12. _____
3. _____	8. _____	13. _____
4. _____	9. _____	14. _____
5. _____	10. _____	15. _____

VIII. REVERSED LETTERS (for example, *tragedy*—spelled by error with the *g* and *d* in exchanged places)

1. _____	6. _____	11. _____
2. _____	7. _____	12. _____
3. _____	8. _____	13. _____
4. _____	9. _____	14. _____
5. _____	10. _____	15. _____

IX. PENMANSHIP (for example, *receive*—scrawled with the *e*'s looking like *i*'s, and a bubble floating somewhere above, like a moon over a series of waves)

1. _____	6. _____	11. _____
2. _____	7. _____	12. _____
3. _____	8. _____	13. _____
4. _____	9. _____	14. _____
5. _____	10. _____	15. _____

X. MISCELLANEOUS (for example, *a lot*—spelled by error as one word instead of two)

1. _____   6. _____   11. _____

2. _____   7. _____   12. _____

3. _____   8. _____   13. _____

4. _____   9. _____   14. _____

5. _____   10. _____   15. _____

CONCLUSION OF ANALYSIS

Write summary statements.

1. SELF-DIAGNOSIS (What are your special kinds of faults as well as your good qualities as a speller?)

2. SELF-PRESCRIPTION (How can you keep improving your spelling? What about certain chapters to review; rules; gimmicks; drills; penmanship; pronunciation; closer inspection of written words; use of dictionary; forming new attitudes, etc.?)

Index to Spelling Words

The chapter number of the word is given.

cord, 4
costume, 4
could, 1
couldn't, 15
council, 3
counsel, 3
counselor, 18
counterfeit, 11
courage, 10
courageous, 9
course, 4
cousin, 10
coward, 10
creation, 9
creature, 10
creditable, 18
crises, 8
criticism, 16, 17
cruelty, 10
crutches, 8
c's, 15
curios, 8
curious, 10
curiosity, 16
custom, 4
customer, 10, 17
cyclone, 1

dairy, 3
dammed, 4
damned, 4
daughter, 10
dear, 4
debatable, 18
debater, 18
deceased, 4
deceive, 10, 11
December, 14
decent, 3
decision, 10
deer, 4
deferment, 12
deferred, 12
definite, 10
definitely, 9
delicious, 10
delight, 1
democracy, 16
dependable, 18
deplorable, 18
deport, 7
descent, 3
description, 10
desert, 3
desirable, 18
desirous, 9
desks, 8
desperate, 10, 17
dessert, 3
detestable, 18
device, 3
devise, 3
dew, 4
diagnoses, 8
dialect, 17
diamond, 16
diary, 3
Dickens' novel, 15

dictionary, 7, 10, 17
didn't, 15
difference, 10
digestible, 18
digging, 12
dilemma, 16, 17
diner, 5
dining, 5
dinner, 5
dirigible, 18
disagree, 7
disappear, 7, 10
disappoint, 7
disastrous, 16
discovery, 7
discussion, 7, 10
diseased, 4
disgust, 17
dishes, 8
Disneyland, 14
dissatisfy, 7
dissimilar, 7
dissolve, 7
distrust, 1
divide, 10
divine, 10, 17
divisible, 18
do, 4
doctor, 10, 18
doesn't, 10, 15
dollar, 10
donation, 9
donkeys, 8
dormitory, 17
dozen, 10
drays, 8
dreaming, 12
driver, 18
driving, 9
dropped, 12
dropping, 12
drove east, 14
drowned, 10, 17
drunkenness, 7
dual, 3
due, 4
duel, 3
during, 10
dyeing, 4, 9
dying, 4
dynamos, 8

easily, 10
Easter, 14
Eastern oysters, 14
echoes, 8
edible, 18
education, 10
effect, 3
efficient, 11
egos, 8
eight, 11
eighth, 17
8's, 15
either, 11
elevator, 18
eligible, 18
elves, 8

embargoes, 8
embryos, 8
emigrate, 4
eminent, 4
emitted, 12
emitting, 12
Empire State
    Building, 14
employer, 18
enemies, 8
energy, 1
engine, 16
English, 14
envelop, 4
envelope, 4
enviable, 18
environment, 10, 17
equipment, 17
equipped, 12
equipping, 12
error, 16
escape, 10, 17
Eskimos, 8
especially, 17
everybody, 10
everybody's, 15
everyone's, 15
everything, 17
exaggerate, 16
excellent, 17
except, 2
excitable, 9, 18
excitement, 9
excusable, 18
exercise, 18
exhilarate, 17
existence, 16, 17
expandable, 18
explanation, 17
extraordinary, 7
extremely, 9

Fahrenheit, 11
fair, 4
fallacy, 16
familiar, 17
families, 8
famous, 9
fare, 4
farmer's wife, 15
farmers' wives, 15
fascinate, 16
fashionable, 18
fastened, 12
fated, 5
Father and
    Mother, 14
fatted, 5
feasible, 18
February, 10, 17
feign, 11
fibber, 5
fiber, 5
field, 11
fiend, 11
fight, 1
finally, 17
financier, 11

fitness, 12
flagged, 12
flappable, 12
flashed, 12
flattest, 12
flea, 4
flee, 4
flew southwest, 14
flexible, 18
flipped, 12
Florida, 14
flour, 4
flower, 4
flushed, 12
folios, 8
fools, 8
foreign, 11
foreigner, 18
foreword, 3
forfeit, 11
formerly, 17
forth, 3
forty, 17
forward, 3
fought, 1
foul, 4
fourth, 3
fowl, 4
Francis' beard, 15
freight, 11
friendly, 10
furthering, 12
future, 16

gasoline, 17
ghettos, 8
ghost, 17
giant, 1
gild, 4
girls' dormitory, 15
glasses, 8
God, 14
government, 7, 17
governor, 7, 18
grabbed, 12
grammar, 10, 17,
    18
grandfather, 17
grasped, 12
grease, 17
Greek gods, 14
greener, 12
grief, 11
griefs, 8
grievous, 17
griping, 5
gripped, 12
gripping, 5
grocery, 1
group, 13
guarantee, 13
guild, 4
gulfs, 8

halves, 8
happiness, 13
have, 4
having, 9

headache, 13
heal, 4
health, 13
Health Education 1A,
    14
hear, 4
heated, 12
heaven, 13
heel, 4
height, 11, 17
heinous, 11
heir, 11
here, 4
heroes' deeds, 15
heroes, 8
heroic, 7
heroism, 7
hers, 15
hindrance, 16
his, 15
history, 14
his uncle, 14
hoarse, 4
hole, 4
holey, 4
holy, 4
"Home on the
    Range," 14
hopeless, 9
hoping, 5, 9
hopping, 5
horrible, 18
horse, 4
hotly, 12
hotter, 12
huge, 1, 4
Hugh, 4
humor, 18
hundred, 13, 17
hungry, 13
hygiene, 11
hypocrisy, 16, 17
hypotheses, 8

ideas, 8
igloos, 8
"I'll be leavin'," 15
I'm, 15
immature, 7
immigrate, 4
imminent, 4
immodest, 7
immoral, 7
imperfect, 7
important, 7
incidence, 4
incidents, 4
incredible, 13, 18
indelible, 18
independent, 13, 17
indescribable, 18
Indians, 14
indivisible, 18
inevitable, 18
ingredient, 16
instance, 4
instants, 4
instead, 3